UC Berkeley
Berkeley, California

Written by Christine Huang and Tak Sato

Edited by Adam Burns and Meryl Sustarsic

Layout by Jon Skindzier

Additional contributions by Omid Gohari, Christina Koshzow, Chris Mason, Joey Rahimi, and Luke Skurman

ISBN # 1-4274-0155-1
ISSN # 1552-0870
© Copyright 2006 College Prowler
All Rights Reserved
Printed in the U.S.A.
www.collegeprowler.com

Last updated 5/16/06

Special Thanks To: Babs Carryer, Andy Hannah, LaunchCyte, Tim O'Brien, Bob Sehlinger, Thomas Emerson, Andrew Skurman, Barbara Skurman, Bert Mann, Dave Lehman, Daniel Fayock, Chris Babyak, The Donald H. Jones Center for Entrepreneurship, Terry Slease, Jerry McGinnis, Bill Ecenberger, Idie McGinty, Kyle Russell, Jacque Zaremba, Larry Winderbaum, Roland Allen, Jon Reider, Team Evankovich, Lauren Varacalli, Abu Noaman, Mark Exler, Daniel Steinmeyer, Jared Cohon, Gabriela Oates, David Koegler, and Glen Meakem.

UC Berkley Bounce-Back Team: Dominic Bocci, Zephyr Drrano, and Hunter Jackson

College Prowler®
5001 Baum Blvd.
Suite 750
Pittsburgh, PA 15213

Phone: 1-800-290-2682
Fax: 1-800-772-4972
E-Mail: info@collegeprowler.com
Web Site: www.collegeprowler.com

College Prowler® is not sponsored by, affiliated with, or approved by UC Berkeley in any way.

College Prowler® strives faithfully to record its sources. As the reader understands, opinions, impressions, and experiences are necessarily personal and unique. Accordingly, there are, and can be, no guarantees of future satisfaction extended to the reader.

© Copyright 2006 College Prowler. All rights reserved. No part of this work may be reproduced or transmitted in any form or by any means, including but not limited to, photocopy, recording, or any information storage and retrieval systems, without the express written permission of College Prowler®.

Welcome to College Prowler®

During the writing of College Prowler's guidebooks, we felt it was critical that our content was unbiased and unaffiliated with any college or university. We think it's important that our readers get honest information and a realistic impression of the student opinions on any campus—that's why if any aspect of a particular school is terrible, we (unlike a campus brochure) intend to publish it. While we do keep an eye out for the occasional extremist—the cheerleader or the cynic—we take pride in letting the students tell it like it is. We strive to create a book that's as representative as possible of each particular campus. Our books cover both the good and the bad, and whether the survey responses point to recurring trends or a variation in opinion, these sentiments are directly and proportionally expressed through our guides.

College Prowler guidebooks are in the hands of students throughout the entire process of their creation. Because you can't make student-written guides without the students, we have students at each campus who help write, randomly survey their peers, edit, layout, and perform accuracy checks on every book that we publish. From the very beginning, student writers gather the most up-to-date stats, facts, and inside information on their colleges. They fill each section with student quotes and summarize the findings in editorial reviews. In addition, each school receives a collection of letter grades (A through F) that reflect student opinion and help to represent contentment, prominence, or satisfaction for each of our 20 specific categories. Just as in grade school, the higher the mark the more content, more prominent, or more satisfied the students are with the particular category.

Once a book is written, additional students serve as editors and check for accuracy even more extensively. Our bounce-back team—a group of randomly selected students who have no involvement with the project—are asked to read over the material in order to help ensure that the book accurately expresses every aspect of the university and its students. This same process is applied to the 200-plus schools College Prowler currently covers. Each book is the result of endless student contributions, hundreds of pages of research and writing, and countless hours of hard work. All of this has led to the creation of a student information network that stretches across the nation to every school that we cover. It's no easy accomplishment, but it's the reason that our guides are such a great resource.

When reading our books and looking at our grades, keep in mind that every college is different and that the students who make up each school are not uniform—as a result, it is important to assess schools on a case-by-case basis. Because it's impossible to summarize an entire school with a single number or description, each book provides a dialogue, not a decision, that's made up of 20 different topics and hundreds of student quotes. In the end, we hope that this guide will serve as a valuable tool in your college selection process. Enjoy!

OMID GOHARI ○ CHRISTINA KOSHZOW ○ CHRIS MASON ○ JOEY RAHIMI ○ LUKE SKURMAN ○
Founders of College Prowler

UC BERKELEY
Table of Contents

By the Numbers............................ **1**	Drug Scene................................ **96**
Academics **4**	Campus Strictness **100**
Local Atmosphere **11**	Parking....................................... **104**
Safety & Security **17**	Transportation **109**
Computers................................ **23**	Weather **115**
Facilities...................... **28**	Report Card Summary **119**
Campus Dining.......................... **34**	Overall Experience **120**
Off-Campus Dining **41**	The Inside Scoop..................... **125**
Campus Housing **48**	Finding a Job or Internship **129**
Off-Campus Housing................ **57**	Alumni **132**
Diversity..................................... **62**	Student Organizations............ **135**
Guys & Girls............................... **68**	The Best & Worst..................... **136**
Athletics..................................... **74**	Visiting....................................... **138**
Nightlife..................................... **82**	Words to Know........................ **143**
Greek Life **90**	

Introduction from the Author

"The most bang for your buck"—this one phrase sums up the University of California, Berkeley. Anybody who has considered a serious higher education in the United States has heard of UC Berkeley; its influential role in both the academic and "real" world is indisputable, and its unique campus history and atmosphere are unlike any other public institution's. With a reputation as being a strangely–brewed microcosm of laid-back liberalism infused with hard-core work ethic, Cal (as Berkeley is affectionately known as) usually invokes a strong reaction from people inside and outside of the community, whether it be pride, disdain, amusement, or bewilderment.

In the minds of Berkeley–lovers, Cal has long stood as a scepter of public education, and perhaps on a more grandiose scale, a testament to American freedom and progressivism. Home to the Free Speech Movement forty years ago, the Affirmative Action debate more recently, and countless other political and social reform movements that have found solace in its open-minded atmosphere, Berkeley has been a harbinger of shifts in American public education policy, as well as larger cultural and political trends.

Berkeley is also a school rich in self-made history; it was the first University of California campus to be built, it has one of the most diverse campuses in the nation, and it ranks continuously as the number one public education choice for students in the United States. Through its constant production of ground-breaking research and innovative thinking in the social and physical sciences, Berkeley has earned the respect of academians, policy-makers, activists, and everyday people all over the world. The education and research opportunities at Cal match, if not surpass, those found at lauded private institutions; but while private-school kids are freezing their pants off on the East Coast for forty grand a year, Berkeleyans are jangling their extra pocket change and constantly smiling at their view of sun-drenched San Francisco.

But beyond all the repute and historical hoopla, Cal has a story that only its students know—a vibe felt only by those who have been inside the "Berkeley Bubble." Demanding professors, unique students, relentless protests—this is all what we Bears have come to expect.

Christine W. Huang, Author
University of California, Berkeley

By the Numbers

General Information

UC Berkeley
110 Sproul Hall
Berkeley, CA 94720

Control:
Public

Academic Calendar:
Semester

Religious Affiliation:
None

Founded:
1868

Web Site:
www.berkeley.edu

Main Phone:
(510) 642-6000

Admissions Phone:
(510) 642-3175

Student Body

Full-Time Undergraduates:
21,771

Part-Time Undergraduates:
1,109

Full-Time Male Undergraduates:
10,535

Full-Time Female Undergraduates:
12,345

Admissions

Overall Acceptance Rate:
25%

Total Applicants:
36,580

Total Acceptances:
9,003

Freshman Enrollment:
3,672

Yield (% of admitted students who actually enroll):
41%

Early Decision Available?
No

Early Action Available?
No

Regular Decision Deadline:
November 30

Regular Decision Notification:
March 31

Must-Reply-By Date:
May 1

Transfer Applications Received:
10,376

Transfer Applications Accepted:
2,584

Transfer Students Enrolled:
1,737

Transfer Application Acceptance Rate:
25%

Common Application Accepted?
No

Supplemental Forms?
No

Admissions E-Mail:
ouars@berkeley.edu

Admissions Web Site:
www.universityofcalifornia.edu/admissions

SAT I or ACT Required?
SAT Required

SAT I Range (25th–75th Percentile):
1200–1450

SAT I Verbal Range (25th–75th Percentile):
580–710

SAT I Math Range (25th–75th Percentile):
620–740

Retention Rate:
96%

Top 10% of High School Class:
99%

Application Fee:
$40

SAT II Requirements:
Two subject tests: Writing and Mathematics Level I, IC, or IIC. One other test in the following subjects: English Literature, Foreign Language, Science, or Social Studies.

Engineering applicants are recommended to take the Mathematics Level IIC test and a third subject test in a Physical Science.

Financial Information

In-State Tuition:
$6,413

Out-of-State Tuition:
$24,233

Room and Board:
$12,554

Books and Supplies:
$1,267

Average Need-Based Financial Aid Package:
$14,361

Students Who Applied for Financial Aid:
62%

Students Who Received Financial Aid:
51%

Financial Aid Forms Deadline:
March 2

Financial Aid Phone:
(510) 642-6442

Financial Aid E-Mail:
fao_ugr@berkeley.edu

Financial Aid Web Site:
http://uga.berkeley.edu/fao

Academics

The Lowdown On...
Academics

Degrees Awarded:
Bachelor
Post-Bachelor's Certificate
Master
Post-Master's Certificate
First Professional
Doctorate

Most Popular Majors:
7% Political Science
6% English
6% Economics
5% Engineering
4% Psychology

Undergraduate Schools:
College of Chemistry
College of Engineering
College of Environmental Design
College of Letters & Sciences
College of Natural Resources
Haas School of Business
The Richard & Rhoda Goldman School of Public Policy
School of Information Management and Systems
School of Public Health

(Undergraduate Schools, continued)
School of Social Welfare
Sargent College of Health and Rehabilitation Sciences
University Professors Program

Graduation Rate:
Four-Year: 53%
Five-Year: 83%
Six-Year: 87%

Full-Time Faculty:
1,442

Faculty with Terminal Degree:
99%

Student-to-Faculty Ratio:
16:1

Average Course Load:
15 units

Best Places to Study:
Free Speech Movement Café
Gardner Main Stacks
Moffitt Undergraduate Library

Special Degree Options
Double/Simultaneous Major option, Inter-UC Visitors Program, Education Abroad Program

AP Test Score Requirements
Possible credit for scores of 3 or above, but specific tests vary by school

IB Test Score Requirements
Possible credit for scores of 5, 6 or 7

Sample Academic Clubs
Asian Business Association, Electrical Engineering Association, African American Business Association, Cal Robotics, Engineers in Medicine and Biology Society, Pre-Med Perspective, Student Organic Gardening Association

Did You Know?

Despite Berkeley's reputation for having huge, over-impacted classes, only 15 percent of the courses offered have **50 or more students**.

Students Speak Out On...
Academics

"The staff at Berkeley is second to none and includes numerous Nobel Prize winners. In most of my classes, I've been impressed with my professors' abilities, but I have heard tales of bad professors."

Q "Excellent! With the exception of one or two professors, I've learned so much from professors here at Cal. Despite what people say, you don't have to be 'just a number' once you come to a large public university like Berkeley. If you make the effort to get to know your professors, you'll find that they're genuinely interested in your academic growth, and they're pretty nice people, too! Generally, **professors in your first and second years will be less personal and harsher graders,** only because the classes are large and they want to 'weed people out.' Once you start your core major classes in junior year, that's when the awesome teaching begins."

Q "As a rhetoric major, I feel like I've had a very special experience at Cal. As opposed to a lot of the science and engineering majors I know, **I've felt connected and interested in nearly every class** I've taken and every professor I've spoken with. My education has been little affected by the size of Cal because my department is smaller than most. Once you find out what you want to focus on academically, Berkeley becomes a lot more manageable."

Q "The teachers are amazing. I have not had any problems approaching my teachers. I've gone to all their office hours just to meet them and make associations, and they love it. Many are foreign. All of mine have been aware of their thick accents and try their best to speak slowly. They will gladly repeat anything. Most of the teachers are published; a lot of the time you end up reading their works or the works by other professors on campus. **A lot of professors are world-renowned scientists and researchers**. There has never, in the history of man, been a better collection of minds in one place at one time, seriously."

Q "Go to class! I think if there is one thing I wish someone had drilled into my head when I came here, it would be that. The teachers are amazing, but you really don't get to see that unless you **go to class as much as possible**. Believe me, I know that sleeping in or having an extra long lunch hour will be awfully tempting at times, but try to get your butt in class—you will be glad you did most of the time, and you'll also feel better about not wasting your parents' money."

Q "Cal's classes are set up in lecture-discussion format. Lecture is the larger class—two to three times a week—with the renowned professor who might have won a Nobel Prize or something. Discussion is with 20-25 students—one to two times a week—with a graduate student instructor (GSI). That way, you get the brilliant instructors and the hands-on attention. However, **There are good professors and GSIs, and bad ones**."

Q "So far, my experience with professors and GSIs has been great. I had an amazing lecturer in an English course last year, but an even more impressive section leader. The lectures gave me an overview of what we were reading and general ideas, and the discussion sections helped me understand the lectures and the readings more. Though **some of my friends at smaller schools criticize the need for smaller discussion sections**, all of my GSIs have been extremely informed and helpful, so I think I've actually gained a lot from the big-school system."

Q "**Most of the professors I've had here have been interesting and inspiring**, but I've also had a couple of duds. The good ones are the ones who talk to students after class, have open office hours, and who try to make their lectures captivating and thought-provoking. The bad ones are the opposite of all that—they sometimes seem to hate lecturing and are impatient with students' questions. Luckily, you can usually tell in the first couple of weeks which one you've got, so you still have time to get out."

The College Prowler Take On...
Academics

The majority of students at Cal agree upon one remarkable aspect of Berkeley that surpasses all else: its enriching academics. After talking to students from a wide variety of departments ranging from philosophy to physics, dance to electrical engineering, every student had at least a few positive things to say about their studies, whether it was an inspiring class they took or a provocative professor they worked with. Nobel Prize-winning lecturers and GSIs with the zeal to match are the norm here. You'll also find ambitious (and somewhat competitive) students who strive to someday experience their instructors' academic recognition. Of course, Berkeley is not free of the few notoriously boring, mean, unapproachable professors who may make your semester feel like an eternity, but they are rare and definitely survivable.

Berkeley is consistently ranked as the number one public University in the United States for several reasons, but perhaps the most dominant one is its challenging academic atmosphere. The intense learning environment in some classes can lead to a high level of anxiety and distrust among students. The massive number of classes and majors may leave students a bit confused, but these cases are exceptions, not the rule. Taking the initiative to research and ask questions about your choices will most definitely quell your anxiety.

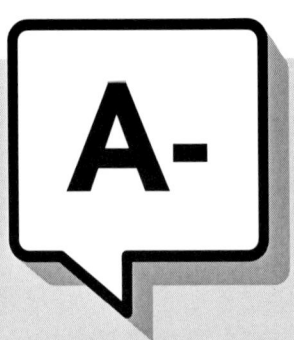

The College Prowler® Grade on
Academics: A-

A high Academics grade generally indicates that professors are knowledgeable, accessible, and genuinely interested in their students' welfare. Other determining factors include class size, how well professors communicate, and whether or not classes are engaging.

Local Atmosphere

The Lowdown On...
Local Atmosphere

Region:
Northern California

City, State:
Berkeley, CA

Setting:
Urban college town

Distance from San Francisco:
20 minutes by car, 40 minutes by BART (mass transit system)

Distance from San José:
1 hour by car

Distance from Lake Tahoe:
4 hours by car

Distance from Santa Cruz:
1.5 hours by car

Closest Movie Theaters:

AMC Bay Street 16
5614 Shellmound St.,
Emeryville
(510) 457-4262

Shattuck Cinemas
2230 Shattuck Ave.,
Berkeley
(510) 843-3456

United Artists Cinemas 7
2274 Shattuck Ave.,
Berkeley
(510) 843-3892

United Artists Emery Bay 10
6330 Christie St.,
Emeryville
(510) 420-0107

Major Sports Teams:

Golden State Warriors (basketball)
Oakland Athletics (baseball)
Oakland Raiders (football)
San Francisco Giants (baseball)

Points of Interest:

Bay Street, Emeryville
Berkeley Rose Garden
Broadway Plaza, Walnut Creek
College Avenue
Telegraph Avenue
Tilden Regional Park

City Web Sites

www.bestofberkeley.com
www.craigslist.org
www.eastbayexpress.com
www.sfbg.com
www.sfstation.com

Did You Know?

5 Fun Facts about Berkeley:
- It was one of the settings for famous writer Jack Kerouac's **Dharma Bums**.
- Many **radioactive elements** were discovered in Berkeley; one has been named Berkelium.
- Berkeley's computer science departments led the **UNIX revolution** in the 1980s.
- Historians cite Berkeley as the spot where the **free speech movement** began in 1964.
- The city and campus have been **featured in movies** like *The Hulk*, *The Graduate*, and *Boys and Girls*.

Famous Berkeley People:

Patty Hearst – Heiress who was kidnapped from Berkeley by the Symbionese Liberation Army in '74

Maxine Hong Kingston – Chinese American writer

Mario Savio – Leader of the free speech movement at Berkeley in '64

Local Slang:

Ghetto – Falling apart, in bad condition

Hella - A lot, really

Hater – Someone who is always saying negative things

Off-the-hook – Awesome, really neat

Students Speak Out On...
Local Atmosphere

> "If you like the outdoors, Berkeley is definitely one of the best places to go to school. It's so close to the ocean, the mountains, woodlands—the weather from spring to early fall is sublime."

Q "Berkeley is much more college town than most people think. There are certain stores and restaurants that everyone know about and go to, and certain aspects of the town that everyone complains about or loves. **After a few years, most students have the place figured out**: They can't give money to every homeless person, or they'll go broke. Crazy people will always be on the bus and are best left alone. And it's impossible to get any studying done anywhere but the library."

Q "**Berkeley has definite atmosphere**. On Telegraph Avenue, street vendors sell their goods on temporary stands. On the weekend, this attracts a lot of people; it's one of the main tourist attractions in Berkeley. Telegraph Avenue has a lot of cool record shops, especially Amoeba Records; it has a very wide selection. I can find things there that I can't find anywhere else, even at most independent record stores. The campus itself is pretty nice. There's a stream running through it, and it has nice landscaping."

Q "San Francisco is where my friends and I go to hang out and party because, unless you're in a frat or sorority, the town is pretty much dead. Sure, there are places to shop and eat and socialize, but they get old fast, and you get sick of seeing your classmates and GSIs everywhere you go. **The culture in SF is a lot more genuine, a lot more true to real life**."

Q "**People are always talking about getting out of the East Bay** and going to SF to do fun things, but I've discovered a lot of cool places to go in Berkeley and Oakland, too. And it's a lot more convenient to hang around locally than riding BART to the city, or driving and going around in circles to find parking."

Q "Berkeley is an interesting place in itself. **Students pretty much dominate the area**, but people love to visit and walk up and down Telegraph—a street bordering campus that has smoke shops, Bohemian people selling trinkets, book stores, coffee and sandwich shops, and thrift stores."

Q "Berkeley is definitely the kind of place you can roll out of bed, rub your eyes, walk to class, and no one will say a thing. There are so many different characters on the street and in your classes. **It's pretty much impossible to judge anyone as unusual** because there will definitely be someone weirder around the corner. I like that people are generally less concerned with clothes, appearances, and showing off money. It makes it easier for school and extra-curricular accomplishments to stand out."

Q "I came from a suburb in Southern California, so Berkeley was shocking to me when I first got here. I wasn't used to stepping over bums on my way to class and **being surrounded by people all my age**."

The College Prowler Take On...
Local Atmosphere

It may seem surprising to hear people refer to Berkeley as a "college town." At a school so large, you might not expect people to feel like they're regulars every place they go. Yet with its relatively limited number of quality places to hang out, study, and eat, this reputation makes sense. For some people, it's a good thing. With a school as large as Berkeley, the feeling of closeness in the community is a nice counterbalance. But for others, the closeness is more of a nuisance than a true benefit. While you may see the same people on your way to school everyday, they're often people you don't know by name, or people you want to avoid.

The city of San Francisco is a nice escape from the college town doldrums; it's a necessary reminder of what the world outside of the "Berkeley Bubble" is like. If you manage your time well, going to the city (or anywhere outside of Berkeley) doesn't have to be an all-day affair, and you can fit this breather in easily between class, studying, and extra-curricular activities. Getting outside of Berkeley's altered reality is not only good for your social well-being, but it is helpful for maintaining your grasp on the more moderate outside world.

The College Prowler® Grade on
Local Atmosphere: B+

A high Local Atmosphere grade indicates that the area surrounding campus is safe and scenic. Other factors include nearby attractions, proximity to other schools, and the town's attitude toward students.

Safety & Security

The Lowdown On...
Safety & Security

Number of UC Berkeley Police:
77

UC Berkeley Police Phone:
911 or (510) 642-3333 from cellular phones

Safety Services:
Night escort service: (510) 642-WALK

Night shuttle service around city & campus: (510) 642-5149

Self-defense courses through UCB

Health Services:
Tang Center: (510) 642-2000

Health Center Office Hours: Monday–Friday: 8 a.m.–6 p.m., Saturday 9 a.m.–5 p.m., closed Sundays and holidays

Did You Know?

The **last reported homicide** on the Berkeley Campus was in 1992.

Students Speak Out On...
Safety & Security

"The University has some safety services, like a nighttime shuttle and safety escorts whom you can call anytime from sundown to 3 a.m. They'll meet you and walk with you to wherever you want to go."

Q "Berkeley is an urban campus, so there are many non-students around. Also, the City of Berkeley is known for its counterculture population—it's hard to get used to, but it really is safe. I haven't known anyone who has been attacked. You just have to get used to ignoring some people. **As long as you don't walk alone, you'll be just fine**. In fact, on many occasions, many of my friends and I have walked home alone from the bars late at night with no problem."

Q "**The campus has many different types of services to make you feel as safe as possible**. There are nighttime shuttles that have door-to-door service, and there's also a program that uses 642-WALK, which will send a person to meet you at any destination and walk you to your home."

Q "**I find security to be pretty good on campus**. Personally, I find Berkeley to be a relatively safe place. There is crime, but I don't see it that often. I feel secure walking alone anytime at night, though it's probably not the wisest idea. So I guess I feel it's secure, but not necessarily perfectly safe."

Q "Inside campus, it's quite safe, and my female friends do not feel threatened. Campus paths are well lit, and we have a good night walking program and lots of security. Around campus, the city of Berkeley is a bit ghetto, and although I personally have never felt threatened before, I've heard stories of people getting harassed. **For girls, it's definitely not a place to walk around alone at night**. If you're with friends, though, it's not too bad."

Q "Well, the campus of UC Berkeley is directly downtown of the city of Berkeley. Safety is an issue sometimes, but the city and the student government are helping to ensure the safety of students by installing lights and blue-light phones to call for police. **The campus does have its own police department**, the UCPD. While safety is not the greatest, it's safe enough to walk around without fear."

Q "I lived in the Unit 1 dorms freshmen year and experienced few safety problems. There are students who sit at the front desk in the lobby who check IDs, call residents down to sign in guests, and report suspicious behavior to the UCPD. It was a pain at the time, but looking back on it, it was a really good way to keep the crime down. My CD player got stolen once from the dining commons, but I think it was my fault because I left my bag unattended. Like anywhere else, **you just have to take care of yourself** and you should be fine."

Q "My parents were worried about sending me off to Berkeley because of its reputation as being kind of sketchy. I was scared here at first, too, but after I learned to watch out for myself by never walking alone late at night, and avoiding carrying a lot of valuables or money, I felt pretty safe. **Living off campus has definitely made me more cautious** because there isn't the extra safety barrier that the school provides in the dorms."

Q "There are lots of services that Berkeley provides for people who are walking home from the library late at night or who need to get around Berkeley at 1 a.m. or something, but **most people I know don't really use the services**. I think it's a macho thing with my guy friends, and it's general laziness for both girls and guys. Once you walk home alone a couple times without running into trouble, you start taking it for granted and think that you're immune to danger. It's stupid, but that's what students assume, sometimes."

Q "Berkeley is really aware of its crime problem and has done a lot to make students feel safe. Yeah, there are a lot of weird people on the streets, but they're usually harmless and keep to themselves. On campus itself, you shouldn't feel too scared. It's pretty sheltered and 99 percent of the people walking around are either students or faculty. Then again, don't just think the non-students are the ones that are threatening. **I know more people who've gotten their things stolen on campus than off**, and a lot of the violence you hear about involves frat boys or stupid kids at bars."

Q "**I got mugged when I was skateboarding in North Berkeley in the middle of the afternoon**. Three high school kids came up to me on an elementary school campus and started asking me questions about my skateboard. They asked if they could try it. I said no, so they surrounded me and beat me up, knocking me out by hitting me on my head with my board. I'll admit that I could've gotten away earlier but I didn't want to seem afraid, so I stayed. It was so messed up; I only had eight dollars on me."

The College Prowler Take On...
Safety & Security

Students concur that UC Berkeley has gone to great lengths to make its students feel safe. Between the night safety shuttles, which run on campus and to places in close proximity to it, the free and convenient night escort service, the several blue-light posts around campus that denote emergency call-boxes, and the high visibility of UCPD throughout the city, most students feel protected. However, some students choose to ignore these services and leave themselves somewhat vulnerable to crime and violence. Students generally find Berkeley sketchy in some areas (downtown and near outlying cities, for example) but only a few students reported crimes committed against them and less then a handful of the crimes were more serious than theft.

If every student used the services provided by Cal, there would most likely be a substantial decrease in crime, and Berkeley's reputation as a dangerous place would change. But only a small percentage of students take advantage of the UC-sponsored safety programs, leaving the general feeling of security somewhat low. So when you get here, walk in groups whenever possible, always lock your doors, try to avoid solicitors, and stay away from places that give you a bad feeling. Though it may seem like a college town at times, Berkeley is nevertheless an urban area, and students should act with caution and conscientiousness.

The College Prowler® Grade on
Safety & Security: B-

A high grade in Safety & Security means that students generally feel safe, campus police are visible, blue-light phones and escort services are readily available, and safety precautions are not overly necessary.

Computers

The Lowdown On...
Computers

High-Speed Network?
Yes, UC Berkeley Campus Network has a T1 connection in all dorms and labs.

Wireless Network?
Yes; 1-day loans for wi-fi cards are also available at Moffitt Library

Number of Labs:
11 labs, 500 computers

Operating Systems:
Mac OS 9 and X; Windows 95, 98, ME, and XP Home

Free Software:
Berkeley offers some free software, including Internet browsers and virus protection. For a complete list, visit their Web site at *http://software.berkeley.edu*.

24-Hour Labs
The computing facility in Heller Lounge

Charge to Print?
Yes; $12 for 200 single-sided, black and white pages

Did You Know?

Most electrical engineering, computer science, and some other physical, biological, and social science **lectures are available to watch** anytime on the Web.

Students Speak Out On...
Computers

"There are always computers available; our computer labs are very good. I do suggest bringing a computer; sometimes you have to pull all-nighters, and it's more convenient to have a computer in your room."

Q "The dorms and campus are both equipped with T1 lines which run pretty fast—**way better than my dial up at home**, at least! Whenever I visit the computer labs, there's usually space to work in. Most people seem to have their own computers."

Q "Berkeley contributed to the growth of Silicon Valley, and high-tech companies give generously, so we have abundant computing resources. Although, labs do get crowded close to finals or midterms. **All the dorms and libraries are connected to the campus high-speed Ethernet**, so I'd definitely recommend bringing a computer with you. However, it's okay if you don't."

Q "**There are always accessible computer labs around campus**, with one in almost every department. I'd say bring your own so that you can use it for fun, as well as academics."

Q "Since coming to Berkeley, I've totally become a laptop-lover! With **Berkeley's AirBears wireless network**, you can sometimes get a signal with your laptop in lecture halls and at nice outdoor spots on campus. It has totally changed my life! Now I feel connected all the time, and e-mailing and research is a lot easier. Printing can be a hassle in the computer labs, though."

Q "Last semester, I literally had to run to turn in a final paper because there was a humungous line for the computers. **During off-season, there usually isn't a huge wait for computers**, except for maybe in the popular labs like Moffitt, Wheeler, and Dwinelle. Your best bet is to go to the lesser-known labs, even if they're on the other side of campus; the time it takes for you to walk there is nothing compared to the possible wait time."

Q "Bring a computer; most residences have DSL. All dorms do. The library provides computer facilities, but they tend to get **long wait lines at critical times** during the year, like at midterms, finals, or just after 8 p.m., in general."

Q "I'm an art major, and I spend a lot of time in studio, but I still think having a computer for yourself is really important. If nothing else, it's nice to have access to e-mail to maintain your friend and family contacts. **The Internet will be your cheapest, most convenient diversion from work**."

Q "I only know a few people who didn't bring their own computers to school. If you can afford it, I would definitely recommend it. Research, writing, and communicating with other students and instructors is, without a doubt, much easier when you have your own computer, especially if you're a procrastinator and like to do your work at the last minute. **Depending on getting a seat in the computer lab is super risky**."

Q "**You should probably bring your own computer, no matter what**; having e-mail contact and typing papers are required in most classes. There are dozens of computer labs all over campus; the busier ones have sign-in sheets to ensure a short wait."

The College Prowler Take On...
Computers

Berkeley students are happy with their computing options, though wait lines and stressed students are common in most facilities. An overwhelming number of students suggest bringing your own personal computer to school, preferably a laptop, if you want to stay in convenient contact with your family, friends, and instructors, as well as work on papers and reports at your own leisure. Berkeley has tried to make private and public computing painless by offering high-speed Internet throughout the dorms, in the labs and library, and now through wireless hubs all over campus.

Berkeley is tech-savvy. Most incoming freshmen bring their own computers, but the numerous labs allow you to get by without one. Although owning your own computer isn't a must, research, e-mail, gaming, chatting, and writing are all unbelievably more convenient when you can walk across the room, rather than walk fifteen blocks to the nearest lab (where you will quite possibly have to wait for an open computer). A caveat: computing is addictive, and with your own box of endless entertainment, it's easy to get sidetracked. If this happens to you, it's a good idea to either take your laptop to the library or go down to one of the less crowded labs when you have a big paper or project due.

The College Prowler® Grade on
Computers: B+

A high grade in Computers designates that computer labs are available, the computer network is easily accessible, and the campus' computing technology is up-to-date.

Facilities

The Lowdown On...
Facilities

Student Centers:
Martin Luther King, Jr. Student Union
Student Learning Center

Athletic Center:
Recreational Sports Facility (also known as the RSF)

Libraries:
38 in all, including Moffitt/Doe Library, the "Main Stacks" (Gardner Stacks), Heller Lounge in Eohleman Hall, Jr. Student Union, and Morrison Reading Room

Campus Size:
1,232 acres

Popular Places to Chill:
The Bear's Lair
Faculty Glade
Free Speech Movement Café
Golden Bear Café
Memorial Glade
Sproul Plaza

What Is There to Do on Campus?
- Attend an outdoor concert: Greek Theatre.
- Read in a comfy place: Morrison Reading Room.
- Watch a classic film: Pacific Film Archive or Media Resource Library.
- Play Frisbee or just relax: Memorial Glade.
- Hear an afternoon concert: Morrison Hall.
- See an art exhibit: Berkeley Art Museum.
- See archaeological artifacts: Kroeber Hall Museum of Anthropology.

Bar on Campus?
The Bear's Lair

Coffeehouse on Campus?
Yes; the Free Speech Movement Café, Ramona's Café, Golden Bear Café, the Terrace, and Pat Brown's Grille.

Movie Theater on Campus?
Pacific Film Archive in Wheeler Auditorium (on designated evenings)

Students Speak Out On...
Facilities

"Berkeley doesn't have a central student center like most campuses. Sproul Plaza, the main entrance to campus, serves that role; it's always crowded with folks tabling for clubs or eating their lunch."

Q "The RSF is a pretty hopping place. There are a few weight rooms, which are usually packed from 6 p.m. to close, and a lot of cardio machines, like elliptical trainers, stationary bikes, treadmills, rowing machines, basketball, racquetball, and volleyball courts, and a few exercise rooms that the martial arts clubs and dance teams use sometimes. **It's pretty big compared to the athletic centers I've seen at other colleges**, and access to the RSF also means access to the pools around campus and another gym up at Strawberry Canyon."

Q "Even though it might not seem like it, **Cal is really into upping its athletics** and getting more students into watching and participating in them. They've put a lot of money into maintaining nice stadiums and fields, improving the RSF, and meeting the needs of the many athletes on campus."

Q "I've watched a lot of performances at Zellerbach because a lot of really interesting and famous acts come through here, and a lot of people from all over the area come to our campus to watch them. International dance companies, orchestras, plays, famous speakers—**you can almost always count on something interesting to be at Zellerbach**, at least a few times a month."

Q "Even if you aren't a big-time Cal athlete, you get to take advantage of the nice fields and stadiums if you do intramural sports, or just run the stadium steps. There are many facilities, but it seems like **a surprisingly small number of people use them**, probably because they're busy studying or in the city."

Q "**Berkeley's facilities are good enough**, unless you're looking for only the best. I think unless you came from an extremely wealthy high school, Berkeley's facilities will be a big improvement."

Q "I think our campus is gorgeous. Athletic fields are great, and the libraries are amazing. I think we have the fourth largest system in the nation. **There are great student services**, over 400 clubs on campus, and good technological facilities as well."

Q "One of the reasons I chose Berkeley was because of its facilities. When I visited the campus, I was impressed by the huge, old-school libraries and stadiums, the nice gym, and the modern labs and buildings. **Berkeley's campus resources match its range of academic choices**."

Q "I've worked as a tutor at the Student Learning Center for two semesters. It's a hidden resource for students—not that many people take advantage of it, and most of the people that do are on contract to do it, like athletes. **You can get help for pretty much anything**, from math to essay writing, you just have to go out and find it. Usually, all the help is free."

Q "A lot of people complain about the Tang Center, saying that it takes forever to get seen, and the people that see you are incompetent or mean. I've never had a really bad experience there; I've always been treated carefully and within an hour or hour and a half. I've also gone to the counseling center in the Tang and was really happy with their services. **I would recommend students to get the University Health Insurance plan**, because it makes seeing the doctor a lot less of a pain. You'll probably get sick more often at college than at home, so the insurance plan helps pay for all the medicine you'll have to buy."

Q "I didn't utilize many of the campus facilities (out of my own laziness), but from what I did see, they weren't very bad. The Recreational Sports Facility should have everything students need, but there's a wait for some of the cardio machines during busy hours. I used the library computer lab pretty often. They're pretty helpful there, and you can print out 200 pages for $12. **There's also a tutoring center that's supposed to be really useful** if you need help in your classes."

Q "The only big complaint I have about Berkeley's facilities is the **lack of career services close to Campus**. There's a career library near the Tang Center, but the Career Center is down several blocks on Bancroft from Campus, making it kind of an inconvenience to go."

The College Prowler Take On...
Facilities

From its athletic fields and basketball courts, to its enormous, resource-filled libraries and research laboratories, Berkeley's awesome facilities are some of the most raved-about features of the school. The extensiveness of Berkeley's facilities is undeniable, and their aesthetic appeal is almost unanimously agreed upon. With the several classical-looking buildings and athletic areas balancing out the newly designed ones, Berkeley combines a modern-historic feel on the outside, with the most up-to-date technology and resources on the inside. Berkeley has also found a prominent place in the arts community with its renowned Zellerbach Playhouse that serves as home to some of the most celebrated groups and performers throughout the year.

The only complaint students seem to have about Berkeley's facilities is that the Career Center is too far from campus and fairly inaccessible. With so many academic options in Berkeley's students' hands, it seems imperative that they provide a convenient and accessible Career Center for students to visit early on in their academic career, as well as throughout it. The athletic and research facilities are abundant and more than adequate, but without the proper "after-Berkeley" preparatory resources, many students find themselves anxious about leaving the plushness of Berkeley in their third and fourth years.

The College Prowler® Grade on
Facilities: B+

A high Facilities grade indicates that the campus is aesthetically pleasing and well-maintained; facilities are state-of-the-art, and libraries are exceptional. Other determining factors include the quality of both athletic and student centers and an abundance of things to do on campus.

Campus Dining

The Lowdown On...
Campus Dining

Freshman Meal Plan Requirement?
Yes

Meal Plan Average Cost:
$3,650

Places to Grab a Bite with Your Meal Plan

Cafè 3
2400 Durant Ave.
Food: Breakfast bar, deli bar, sandwiches, soups, desserts
Favorite Dish: Jamaican black bean soup
Hours: Monday–Friday 10 a.m.–2 p.m., Sunday–Thursday 5 p.m.–9 p.m.

Clark Kerr Campus (CKC)
2601 Warring St.

Food: Salads, soups, made-to-order sandwiches, desserts

Favorite Dish: Thai chicken salad

Hours: Monday–Friday 7:15 a.m.–9 a.m., 11 a.m.–1:30 p.m., 5:30 p.m.–8 p.m., Saturday–Sunday 11 a.m.–2 p.m., 5:30 p.m.–8 p.m.

Crossroads
2415 Bowditch St.

Food: Pizza, grill, vegan, deli

Favorite Dish: Hawaiian pizza

Hours: Monday–Friday 7 a.m.–8 p.m., Saturday–Sunday 10 a.m.–3 p.m., 5 p.m.–8 p.m.

The Den
2415 Bowditch St.

Food: Sandwiches, smoothies

Favorite Dish: Mozzarella fresca sandwich

Hours: Daily 7 a.m.–12:30 a.m.

Foothill
2700 Hearst Ave.

Food: Pizza, deli, vegetarian

Favorite Dish: Tomato and feta salad

Hours: Monday–Friday 7:15 a.m.–9:30 a.m., 11 a.m.–1:30 p.m., 5 p.m.–8 p.m., Saturday–Sunday 10:30 a.m.–1:30 p.m., 5 p.m.–8 p.m., 9 p.m.–2 a.m.

Golden Bear Cafè
Cesar Chavez Student Center

Food: Sandwiches, sushi, hamburgers, breakfast, soups

Favorite Dish: Bread bowl soups

Hours: Monday–Thursday 7 a.m.–10 p.m., Friday 7 a.m.–4 p.m., Saturday 10 a.m.–4 p.m., Sunday 12 p.m.–8 p.m.

Pat Brown's
Koshland Hall

Food: Breakfast, sandwiches, sushi, hamburgers

Favorite Dish: Chicken Teriyaki

Hours: Monday–Friday 7:30 a.m.–4 p.m.

Ramona's
Wurster Hall

Food: Breakfast, sushi, made-to-order paninis and rice bowls

Favorite Dish: Chicken lemon tarragon salad

Hours: Monday–Thursday 7:30 a.m.–7 a.m., Friday 7:30 a.m.–4 p.m.

The Terrace
Bechtel Building Rooftop

Food: Breakfast, salads, soups

Favorite Dish: Taco salad

Hours: Monday–Friday 7:30 a.m.–4 p.m.

Other Places to Check Out

The Bear's Lair Pub
2475 Bancroft Way (Student Union)
Food: Pizza, burgers, assorted bar food
Favorite Dish: Rocket burger
Hours: Monday–Wednesday 11:30 a.m.–1 a.m.,
Thursday–Saturday 11:30 a.m.–2 a.m.

The Bear's Lair, a tremendously popular student hangout that's been open since 1962, is located on campus but unaffiliated with the University (and therefore doesn't accept UC Berkeley's meal plan). The bar closed and underwent a well-needed rennovation in 2000, and has since re-opened for business. Though the pub does serve food, it's mostly known as a bar; see the Nightlife section for more information.

Off-Campus Places to Use Your Meal Plan
None

24-Hour On-Campus Eating?
No

Student Favorites
Crossroads, the Den, the Golden Bear Café

Other Options
Cal 1 Debit Card, Cal Diners' Club, Co-operative Housing Room & Board plan

Did You Know?

Even if you're not a hall resident, you can **still use a meal plan** with the Cal 1 Debit Card or the Cal Diners' Club.
Go to *hwww.housing.berkeley.edu/dining/meal_plans.html* for more info.

Students Speak Out On...
Campus Dining

> "Crossroads is the best thing to happen to campus food since I don't know when. I was in the dorms before the dining commons was built, and the food was barely edible."

Q "The incoming freshmen have no idea how big of an improvement Berkeley's new dining options are over the old ones. I used to work at Unit 1's Dining Commons (also known as DCs), so I know how gross the food is. There's a small snack shop inside Crossroads restaurant called the Den. It stays open until 12:30 a.m., later than a lot of restaurants and all of the other DCs, selling drinks, pizzas, baked things, and other snacks."

Q "I really like the new Crossroads dining hall. Almost all dorm residents go there even though a lot of them have their own dining commons. I've been to the other DCs a couple of times, and I have to say that **I'm really lucky to be living across the street from the Crossroads**; it's by far the best meal plan place to go. There's usually a lot of people there, but it's definitely worth it if you have a meal plan."

Q "If you're a freshman, I say **a meal plan with lots of Flex Points is probably the best way to go**. You have the freedom to eat at the dining halls when you feel like it, and other places on and off campus when you don't, without feeling pressured to get your money's worth. A lot of people who don't live in the halls have been joining the Cal Diners' Club. The food's not bad and it's really convenient if you don't cook or if you live by yourself."

Q "The dorm food at Berkeley is horrible. If I lied and told you the food was edible, I'd feel intense guilt. It's not. **Get the smallest meal plan you can**, because most people just end up eating cereal, wilted salads, and frozen yogurt."

Q "Okay, I'm going to be perfectly honest with you. . . **dorm food really sucks**! I mean it's edible, but it isn't great. But after a while you get used to it and you probably won't even notice. There are also several on-campus restaurants that let you use swipes from your ID to buy food. My favorite is the Golden Bear Café because I can use my card there."

Q "**Food on Campus is okay at the Golden Bear Café**, where you can use your meal swipes from the dining commons. There's also the Free Speech Movement Café, which is a great place to study and hang out with friends. There are hundreds of wonderful places to eat just off campus."

Q "I have only eaten in the halls a few times. It depends on the dorm. I think Clark Kerr is decent. **I eat at my sorority, and the food is amazing**. I'm very fortunate to live around the corner from my sorority, so it's way easy for me."

Q "**I love Bear's Lair—it's a campus staple**. I heard it had closed down several years ago, and I'm really glad it re-opened. It serves all sorts of beer, pizzas, salads, and other pub food. It's the only place on campus you can get or drink alcohol, so a lot of the older students and grad students hang out there. It's great to sit on the patio and drink a pitcher with your friends on late afternoons, when you're done with all your classes."

Q "On campus, there are restaurants all run by Housing and Dining. The food there is expensive and okay. **The dorm food is cheap, but less than okay**. You don't come to Berkeley for the food. Around the campus area, there is every kind of food you could possibly imagine, and there are some great restaurants. Of course, nearby San Francisco has more restaurants per capita than nearly any other city in the world."

The College Prowler Take On...
Campus Dining

Nearly every student with a meal plan mentions Crossroads and the Den as good on-campus choices for eating and socializing. The huge, 800-person capacity commons is clean, modern, and gives students more of a buffet-style setting, rather than a cafeteria atmosphere. While many say the food is still not gourmet quality, it's much better than other on-campus choices and provides the convenience of ethnically-diverse fare just across the street from home. The other on-campus restaurants serve less-enticing entrees with less variation, but they are nonetheless good places to grab a quick snack or sip coffee and read. Most students also agree that the meal plan is a good idea for incoming students because it's considerably flexible, convenient, and affordable, and it gives students one less thing to worry about when adjusting to Cal.

While many students seem happy about the recent addition of Crossroads and the recent re-addition of the Bear's Lair to on-campus and residential dining options, many of the students deemed the remaining options as "barely edible." Entrees are bland at best, the vegetables at the salad bar are often discolored, and the rotating menus only exacerbate the situation. The flexibility of the meal plans is a real savior for Berkeley students, while the dining options outside of the dormitories provide real alternatives that many students are quite satisfied with.

The College Prowler® Grade on
Campus Dining: C

Our grade on Campus Dining addresses the quality of both school-owned dining halls and independent on-campus restaurants as well as the price, availability, and variety of food.

Off-Campus Dining

The Lowdown On...
Off-Campus Dining

Restaurant Prowler: Popular Places to Eat!

Blondie's
Food: Pizza
2340 Telegraph Ave.
(510) 548-1129
Cool Features: Huge pizzas, pickup and delivery available.
Price: $8–$10 per person
Hours: Sunday–Monday 11 a.m.–2 a.m., Tuesday–Thursday 11 a.m.–1 a.m., Friday–Saturday 11 a.m.–2 a.m.

Café Intermezzo
Food: Salad
2442 Telegraph Ave.
(510) 849-4592
Cool Features: Salads with the works, bigger than your torso at $5.
Price: $5–$7 per person
Hours: Monday–Sunday 8:45 a.m.–10 p.m.

Fat Slice
Food: Pizza
2375 Telegraph Ave.
(510) 548-6479
Price: $5–$10 per person
Hours: Sunday–Thursday
10 a.m.–12:30 a.m.,
Friday–Saturday
10:30 a.m.–2 a.m.

Gordo Taqueria
Food: Mexican
2989 College Ave.
(510) 204-9027
Cool Features: Best chicken burritos at the cheapest price in Berkeley.
Price: $10–$15 per person
Hours: Daily 10:30 a.m.–12 a.m.

La Burrita
Food: Mexican
2530 Durant Ave.
(510) 845-4859
Price: $15–$20 per person
Hours: Sunday–Thursday
11 a.m.–11 p.m., Friday–Saturday 11 a.m.–1:30 a.m.

La Note Restaurant
2377 Shattuck Ave.
(510) 843-1535
Cool Features: Real french toast!
Price: $15–$20 per person

(La Note Restaurant, continued)
Hours: Sunday–Friday
8 a.m.–2:30 p.m., Friday–Saturday 8 a.m.–10 p.m., Thursday–Saturday 6 p.m.–10 p.m., Saturday–Sunday
8 a.m.–3 p.m.

Shen Hua
Food: Chinese
2914 College Ave.
(510) 883-1777
Cool Features: High-class Chinese food.
Price: $15–$18 per person
Hours: Monday–Saturday
11 a.m.–2:30 p.m., Monday–Friday 5 p.m.–10 p.m.

Top Dog
Food: Hot dogs
2534 Durant Ave.
(510) 643-5967
Price: $3–$7 per person
Hours: Monday–Thursday
10 a.m.–2 a.m., Friday
10 a.m.–3 a.m., Saturday
11 a.m.–3 a.m., Sunday
11 a.m.–2 a.m.

Trattoria La Siciliana
Food: Italian
2993 College Ave.
(510) 704-1474
Cool Features: Chefs are so good, the patrons know their schedules.
Price: $20–$25 per person
Hours: Tuesday–Sunday
5:30 p.m.–10 p.m.

Zachary's Pizza
Food: Pizza
5801 College Ave.
(510) 655-6385

Cool Features: Tomatoes smother the top, cheese and topping underneath! Always a line out the door for dinner.

Price: $8–$12 per person

Hours: Sunday–Thursday 11 a.m.–10 p.m., Friday–Saturday 11 a.m.–10:30 p.m.

Other Places to Check Out:
Blue Nile, Café de la Paz, Chez Panisse, Koryo Sushi, La Mediterranee, Mama's Café, Noah's Bagels

Student Favorites:
Gordo Taqueria, Café Intermezzo, Zachary's Pizza, anywhere on Durant Avenue

Late-Night, Half-Price Food Specials:
Top Dog, La Burrita

24-Hour Eating?
Gordo Taqueria

Closest Grocery Stores:
Safeway
6310 College Ave.
(510) 654-6992

Andronico's
2655 Telegraph Ave.
(510) 845-1280

Whole Foods Market
3000 Telegraph Ave.
(510) 649-1333

Did You Know?

Berkeley's **Farmer's Market** takes place every Thursday, Saturday, and Sunday, all year-round.

San Francisco has the **second most restaurants** per square foot in the U.S., right behind NYC.

We are one hour from **wine country** (Calistoga, Napa Valley, Sonoma).

The restaurant-packed food court on Durant Avenue is colloquially referred to as the **Asian Ghetto**, though this area is not technically a ghetto, and neither is it filled primarily with Asian restaurants.

Students Speak Out On...
Off-Campus Dining

"**Berkeley has almost any kind of food you could want. The areas surrounding campus are pretty lively and have lots of restaurants. You have to try out several, and you'll find some that fit your tastes.**"

Q "People always talk about going to the city to go out to eat, but I think that Berkeley and the surrounding area have so many great options that you should try out things here before heading out there. The food places on the blocks surrounding Berkeley are okay, but **the really good restaurants are the ones that not everyone knows about**, like Koryo Sushi and Mama's Café in Oakland. You've got so many options in the area, and they're probably a lot cheaper than the same quality food you'll find in SF."

Q "The best part of Berkeley is that **there are lots of restaurants with good, cheap food that're open late**. We have Top Dog, which has all kinds of hot dogs and is open until 2 a.m.—it's very useful for post-partying or studying. We also have Fat Slice and Blondie's, two really good pizza places. There's La Burrita, which has great Mexican food, Cafe Intermezzo, where you can get the best salad in the world that's bigger than your head for around five bucks, and a place we call the 'ghetto food court' which has lots of cheap Chinese, Japanese, Thai, Korean, and Mediterranean food."

Q "There are so many great places to eat off campus. You will find whatever type of food you're in the mood for. **Telegraph is so busy all the time**. Basically, all the restaurants you find on and off Telegraph are great."

Q "The restaurants on campus are decent, but the restaurants off campus are really good. The best places to get food close by are on Durant and Telegraph Avenues. Both Fat Slice and Blondie's serve large slices of pizza for a really good price. The 'Asian Ghetto' is like a little food court off Durant that primarily features Asian eateries which are all good. The Asian Ghetto is also home to a pretty good Italian place. **Top Dog is a hot dog stand that serves really good hot dogs**. There are lots of places to eat off campus."

Q "Every time my friends and family visit me up here, they always want to go out to eat because there are so many good restaurants in the area. I've been to restaurants that serve all types of food, from Ethiopian at the Blue Nile, to Brazilian at Café de la Paz. **Everything I've had has been from good to unbelievable**."

Q "The restaurants on College are probably the most popular in the area, at least for older Berkeley students and locals. **One of the best meals I've ever had was at La Mediterranee**, where they served a two-person brunch with every Mediterranean dish you could imagine for a reasonable price. I've also had really nice meals at several of the other restaurants, ranging from pretty expensive, like Shen Hua, to darn cheap, like Gordo's."

Q "People are really missing out if they just stay within the two mile radius of campus when they go out to eat. Some of the best bets are in downtown Berkeley, Albany, Oakland, and Rockridge. I like that you can find pretty much any kind of food at a reasonable price and of decent quality within five or ten miles of Berkeley itself. If you want to drive a little farther, **Mexican food in Fruitvale is really authentic and yummy**."

Q "While **most of my frat brothers and I usually go to the Asian food court and Top Dog** to get our food, there are a lot of other good places farther away from Berkeley, reachable by car or bus. Zachary's Pizza is one of the most talked about and liked restaurants; they serve deep-dish pizza that's covered in tomato sauce and is unbelievably heavy. There's almost always a line out the door at night."

Q "Berkeley is known for having great types of food. We have all types of food on Telegraph, which is our main street. Zachary's pizza is great. There's great Asian food, great Mexican, and so much more. There's nothing like La Burrita or Top Dog at 2 a.m. I love all the sandwich places, as well. Oh, and Noah's Bagels is great. I don't have a car, so it's hard for me to really go check out the rest of the restaurants. If you're going way gourmet, **there's a place called Chez Panisse. It's one of the most famous restaurants here**."

The College Prowler Take On...
Off-Campus Dining

Students at Berkeley are more than satisfied with their off-campus food selection. Ranging from cheap ($3 for a bratwurst with the works at Top Dog) to not so cheap ($75 for a prix-fix meal at Chez Panisse), the food in the Berkeley area almost always lives up to "the hype." With the on-campus food often less than palatable, the endless variety of off-campus dining choices is not only nice, but to some degree necessary. Students agree that there is a cornucopia of places to sit, eat, drink, and socialize, no matter how much money is in your wallet, or what you're in the mood for.

If you live in the dorms and you don't have a car, you'll most likely be sticking with the around-the-corner favorites—Top Dog, La Burrita, Durant Avenue's "ghetto food court," Fat Slice, and Blondie's. But if you are feeling a little sick of the grease and the same crowd every night, then be happy to know that there is still an entire world of cheap, good food just a few more blocks away (sometimes a little more). So skip the dining commons once in a while and head out somewhere a little more risky, maybe somewhere farther than you're used to walking, like College Avenue, University Avenue, or Solano Avenue. You'll build up an appetite that'll definitely be satisfied.

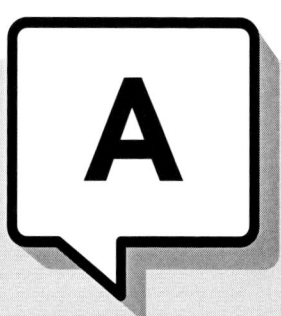

The College Prowler® Grade on
Off-Campus Dining: A

A high Off-Campus dining grade implies that off-campus restaurants are affordable, accessible, and worth visiting. Other factors include the variety of cuisine and the availability of alternative options (vegetarian, vegan, Kosher, etc.).

Campus Housing

The Lowdown On...
Campus Housing

Room Types:
Single, double, triple-person occupancy rooms are offered only in Units 1, 2, and 3.

Quads (4-person) occupancy available only in Bowles Hall.

Some double/triple conjoined with two or three other bedroom suites with shared bathroom and common area.

Best Dorms:
Foothill
Clark Kerr

Worst Dorm:
Stern

Undergrads Living on Campus:
35%

Number of Dormitories:
8

Number of University–Owned Apartments:
Two apartment complexes with housing only available to graduate and law students and UC student families.

Dormitories:

Unit 1
Floors: Four high-rises, eight floors in each
Total Occupancy: 237 per building
Bathrooms: Coed bathrooms shared by floor, single-sex bathrooms shared by floor
Coed: Yes
Room Types: Single, double, triple, triple room suite
Special Features: Single-sex floors, sixteen floor lounges with balconies, main lounge with fireplaces, Security Monitor Program, laundry facilities, dining center, Academic Center with computers, houses the African American theme program

Unit 2
Floors: Four high-rises, eight floors in each
Total Occupancy: 230 per building
Bathrooms: Coed bathrooms shared by floor, single-sex bathrooms shared by floor
Coed: Yes
Room Types: Single, double, triple, triple room suite
Special Features: Single-sex floors available, sixteen floor lounges with balconies, main lounge with fireplace, Academic Center with computers, academic support and tutoring programs, Security Monitor Program, laundry facilities

Unit 3
Floors: Four high-rises, eight floors in each
Total Occupancy: 230 per building
Bathrooms: Coed bathrooms shared by floor, single-sex bathrooms shared by floor
Coed: Yes
Room Types: Single, double, triple, triple room suite
Special Features: Lounges with balconies, main lounge with fireplace, dining center, Academic Center with computers, Security Monitor Program, laundry facilities in central commons building, houses Spens-Black Hall (rooming for upper-division and transfer students)

Bowles
Total Occupancy: 192
Bathroom: Shared by floor
Coed: No
Percentage of Men/Women: 100/0
Room Types: Quad rooms
Special Features: Library, TV lounge, and recreation room, access to Academic Center with computers at Foothill, laundry facilities, also resembles a castle

Clark Kerr Campus

Total Occupancy: 818

Bathrooms: Shared by floor

Coed: Yes, except for suites

Room Types: Single, double, triple-person connected with other singles, doubles, or triples (suites)

Special Features: Single-sex suites with shared bathroom, dining center with outdoor patios, Academic Center with computers, Security Monitor Program, recreation rooms, study lounges, laundry facilities, outdoor pool, sand volleyball, tennis courts, track

College Durant Apartments

Total Occupancy: 120

Percentage of First-Year Students: 0% (graduate and law students only)

Room Types: Two, three, four, five, or six-bedroom apartments

Special Features: Apartments furnished, phone and internet lines provided in bedrooms, common area lounges, study rooms, recreation room, vending machine room, mail room, shared outdoor courtyard, laundry room, bicycle storage

Foothill

Floors: Seven coed buildings

Total Occupancy: 776 total

Bathrooms: Shared by suite

Coed: Yes; in suites with six or more bedrooms

(Foothill, continued)

Room Types: Single, double, triple suites with three to eleven bedrooms

Special Features: Academic Center with computers, dining center in commons building, assembly rooms, TV lounge, mail services, laundry facilities

Manville Apartments

Total Occupancy: 132

Percentage of First-Year Students: 0% (graduate and law students only)

Room Types: Single studio-style apartments, unfurnished

Special Features: Central courtyard, secured entry and elevator, common areas, lounge, laundry facilities, mail room, three study rooms, storage spaces, limited parking spaces available for additional fees.

Stern

Floors: 4

Total Occupancy: 267

Bathroom: Shared by floor

Coed: No

Percentage of Men/Women: 0/100

Room Types: Single, double, double rooms in suites

Special Features: Main lounge with fireplace and grand piano, Security Monitor Program, Academic Center with computers, dining in adjoining Foothill Dining Center

Smyth Fernwald Complex

Total Occupancy: 74 student families

Coed: Yes

Room Types: One, two, or three bedroom apartments

Special Features: Peaceful living environment for student families

University Students' Cooperative Association (co-op)

Floors: 17 buildings with three to four floors

Total Occupancy: 1,200

Bathroom: Shared by floor; shared by apartment

Coed: By building

Room Types: Single, double, some triple rooms; apartments with one to four bedrooms

Special Features: Each house is independently managed by elected house members, and every member contributes work time to running the co-op. There are two co-ops for women only, a vegetarian house, a gay/lesbian/bisexual/transgender theme house, and an African American theme house. One house is reserved for UC Berkeley graduate and re-entry students. For more information, visit their Web site at *www.usca.org*.

University Village, Albany

Total Occupancy: Students with families only

Room Types: 760 one, two and three bedroom apartments, and two-bedroom townhouses

Special Features: Recreational and community center, a café, laundry rooms, and child care center

Bed Type
Twin, Extra-long

Cleaning Service?
Hallway, common room and bathroom cleaning only

What Do You Get In Your Dorm Room?
All rooms are carpeted and include dressers, desks, chairs, bookshelves, general lighting, closets, mirrors, and curtains. Each room has in-room network connections and basic cable. Every hall has a recreation area, laundry facilities, vending/ice machines and live-in health workers and live-in hall staff. All University buildings are designated smoke-free.

Did You Know?

Berkeley is the only UC campus to offer a lesbian/gay/bisexual/transgender-**themed residential program**.

Students Speak Out On...
On-Campus Housing

> "I think the dorms are a very personal matter. It depends on your personality. If you're a social person, I would suggest avoiding Unit 4, which is Foothill, Stern, and Bowles."

Q "I know people that were placed in Foothill, and they found that **many people were not very social**. My friends and I made the best of the situation, and I think that we ended up shaking the place up a little bit. Foothill has awesome rooms, though, and they're all pretty big."

Q "I'd definitely stay away from Stern. It's not cool at all; my friends call it the women's prison. The Units are very fun, but the rooms can be really small. The best is Unit 3, then Unit 1, and Unit 2. There's also Clark Kerr; these dorms are beautiful, but they're a little farther away from campus. They're worth it, though. I would put Clark Kerr as a first choice. But **no matter where you end up, it'll be a positive experience**. It all depends on you."

Q "Dorms are pretty nice. I'd say try for Foothill if you're willing to pay a bit more for comfort. But your meal plan allows you to eat in any dorm dining common, so many people sign up for a cheaper dorm and just eat at the nicer dining places. **Dorms are a great way to meet people and enjoy social life**, especially as a freshman. I'd definitely recommend that you stay in a dorm for at least one year."

Q "I lived in Clark Kerr my first year as a junior transfer, and it was okay, but not really conducive to meeting a lot of new, interesting people, especially my own age. I didn't know this, but CKC is predominantly an athlete dorm. Many of them are recruits and get the hook-ups to the nice living arrangements and, also, because it's so close to a lot of the sports fields. So, at the dining commons, a lot of the teams would just sit with each other and be uninterested in meeting anyone else. **CKC has nice surroundings and is really roomy** compared to the tiny rooms in the Units, but I'd have chosen another place to live if I'd known what most of the residents were like."

Q "Units 1 and 2 are closest to the concentrated Greek scene and equally close to campus. **Kerr has many of the athletes and tends to be pretty social**, along with Unit 1. Foothill is very quiet; it tends to attract more studious types. For reference, if you can find a map, the Greek scene is basically any building within two blocks of the corner of Piedmont and Channing, and a few houses along Bancroft, across from Campus."

Q "If you're willing to pay more . . . Clark Kerr or Foothill are nice places to live, but they're far away! I lived in Unit 3 Residence Hall this past year . . . it was okay. It was only a block away from campus. No matter where you live, there are pros and cons. **You'll make friends no matter what**, though."

Q "Units 1, 2, and 3 are eight-floor, four-building high-rises located on the south side of campus. They contain mostly double and some triple rooms in typical dorm style. Clark Kerr is a spread-out, mission-style set of buildings, about a 25-minute walk from campus. **Rooms there are somewhat more spacious** and are mostly doubles. Foothill and Bowles/Stern are on the north side of campus and contain sets of rooms that share a common area. Bowles is the all-male dorm; Stern is the all-female one. All other dorms are coed, except for certain floors in the Units."

Q "**A lot of people only look into the co-ops their second or third years**, but it's definitely a good option for first-year students and transfers, too. The co-ops are houses of all sizes and themes that are run by the residents. They usually require a certain number of hours of chore work as part of living expenses. Co-ops also include a communal kitchen and house meals and parties, so a lot of people who are on a tight budget but who want a social atmosphere choose the co-ops. I lived at Casa Zimbabwe my second semester here, and it was definitely a learning experience. The larger co-ops, like CZ and Cloyne, are dirtier and less family-like than the smaller ones, but they also give people the chance to meet a huge variety of students and non-students from all over with all sorts of stories and experiences."

Q "**The co-op scene is cool for a while**; it's kind of neat living communally and feeling like you're really working for your room and board, but then when the place gets all trashed at parties, the communal areas become dirty and stinky, and people stop doing a good job on their chores, it's not so fun anymore. People who live in co-ops are kind of cliquish; they have an air of superiority about them because they live in this co-op or that co-op. The food was pretty lousy, too, and I had to go out to eat a lot of the time. Try it out for a semester if you want, but I'd definitely be ready to move out after a year."

Q "Dorms aren't bad at all. Usually it works out kind of give-and-take; **if you have a tiny triple, your roommates or floormates will be cool**. If your room is roomy and nice, your roommates will be duds. Of course this isn't the case all the time, but with my friends, this is often how it turned out."

The College Prowler Take On...
Campus Housing

Students at Cal seem generally pleased with their on-campus housing options. The dorms range from study-oriented (Foothill, Bowles/Stern) to party-producing (Units, CKC), each with their pros and cons, depending on what you consider important in your living situation. Most students were placed in rooms of their preference, and few had seriously harsh remarks about their roommates or resident advisors. Several people cited the co-op system as an interesting, virtually on-campus, alternative to the dormitories, but they also gave a few warnings about their safety, cleanliness, and druggie environments. The co-operative housing system is not directly linked to the University, so many of the health and safety guidelines are not met or consistently monitored.

Whatever you find the most important in your living environment—spacious rooms, cool roommates, nice scenery, campus proximity—there's a dorm room at Cal to fit you. That isn't to say you'll definitely get your top-choice in all those categories, but most likely, your most important needs will be met, and you will live somewhere tolerable, if not totally enjoyable. The best way to avoid dorm room dread is by getting your residential living forms in early, being honest on your forms (and with yourself/your roommate) about your particular living preferences and habits, and going into your new arrangement with a positive attitude and realistic outlook about the possible nuisances of dorm life.

The College Prowler® Grade on
Campus Housing: B

A high Campus Housing grade indicates that dorms are clean, well-maintained, and spacious. Other determining factors include variety of dorms, proximity to classes, and social atmosphere.

Off-Campus Housing

The Lowdown On...
Off-Campus Housing

Undergrads in Off-Campus Housing:
65%

Best Time to Look for a Place:
December–March, if looking for summer/fall housing

Average Rent For:
Studio Apt.: $750–$1,100
1BR Apt.: $900–1,500
2BR Apt.: $1,250–$2,200

Popular Areas:
College Avenue
Hearst Avenue
Oakland
El Cerrito

For Assistance Contact

Cal Rentals
Berkeley's Housing and Dining Office rental service
http://calrentals.housing.berkeley.edu
Phone: (510) 642-3642
E-mail: homeinfo@berkeley.edu

Craig's List
(non-profit)
www.craigslist.org

E-Housing
San Francisco East Bay Area housing
www.ehousing.com
Phone: (510) 549-2000, or (888) 945-RENT
E-mail: info@ehousing.com

Students Speak Out On...
Off-Campus Housing

> "Finding housing off-campus is a struggle because of the competition. My friends and I searched for a while and found an awesome apartment near campus. Housing is hard to find, but not impossible."

💬 "Housing off campus can be a pain. There's a housing crunch because a lot of people want to live here. This means that rent is high, and **you have to put some work in to get an apartment**. The co-op system is also a great alternative, with several houses in town."

💬 "Unfortunately, this is one of the big negatives of Berkeley. Berkeley only offers one year of guaranteed housing. Most of my friends had to get apartments off campus after their first year. The city of Berkeley fights a lot with the University over student housing. They basically stand on the side of the greedy landlords who vote for them, and screw over the students. Of course, there are some good apartments, but **most landlords are just interested in taking as much money as they can** from you. The trick is to start your apartment hunting early so that you have some choice. A lot of my friends eventually found a place that was livable and a reasonable price."

💬 "Finding housing is a long and grueling process, but it's definitely doable if you start early enough and are persistent. **Most of the landlords around here are pretty money-grubbing**, so you really have to be savvy to land a place that is worth what you'll be paying. Don't settle!"

Q "I rushed a sorority because people told me finding housing on my own would be a bigger pain. If you don't have something you've been working on, like a house with five friends or an apartment with two other people, it'll be hard once May rolls around because everyone else already started months ago. **I had a friend who started visiting new places in December**. You really have to keep your eye out for a close, cheap place—and even then, nothing's guaranteed."

Q "**Housing sucks here**. That's one reason to join a frat—easy housing. You really have to work at it; it is expensive. It's not impossible, just hard to do sometimes. You have to remember that the Bay Area is one of the most costly places to live, so that is why it's expensive."

Q "Off-campus housing is convenient because you always know about everything going on. **It is less than a 15-minute walk to most places in Berkeley**, which isn't that bad. Public transportation (BART) isn't too far, so you can escape to the city pretty easily."

Q "I would seriously consider living outside of Berkeley, like in Rockridge, Oakland, Emeryville, or El Cerrito. If you want to live off-campus, you don't want to be scrounging for money all the time. The rent is sometimes half as much once you get out of Berkeley, and a lot of places are filled with students, from Cal and other colleges, and totally accessible by bus or BART. My boyfriend lives in Oakland, and he pays less than $400 for his own room in an awesome house run by artists. He can hop on the bus and be on campus in fifteen minutes. If you're going to use services, like E-housing, definitely **make sure that you're including places beyond Berkeley in your search**; you'll have better luck finding a gem a few bus stops away than right around campus."

The College Prowler Take On...
Off-Campus Housing

The off-campus housing search at Berkeley isn't easy. Students complain about expensive rent, costly utility bills, competitive seekers, and lazy landlords. In addition, few end up in locations to their exact liking, but all say that they're grateful that they even found a place. The demand for housing from the 40,000 undergraduate and graduate students drive up the rent prices to ridiculous levels. Berkeley is very aware of the housing crunch and provides several services to help students in their transition from dorms to apartment life. Many students cite the importance of planning early and at least thinking about post-dorm living options in the early spring (if planning on moving in the early fall; start even earlier if you want to move in at the beginning of summer).

A couple of students said they lucked out and found their places at the last moment, weeks or days before school began. Though you might often see "Roommate Wanted" signs in the bathrooms at school throughout the year, finding a new place to live at the last minute or during the school year is time consuming and adds a lot of mental stress. Try to find people you'd possibly like to live with early on, talk to them about possible plans, and start visiting places as soon as ones that interest you pop up. Try to stop yourself from just committing to the first place that seems "okay" out of laziness or fear that you may have no other options.

The College Prowler® Grade on
Off-Campus Housing: C

A high grade in Off-Campus Housing indicates that apartments are of high quality, close to campus, affordable, and easy to secure.

Diversity

The Lowdown On...
Diversity

African American:
4%

Asian American:
40%

Hispanic:
11%

Native American:
1%

White:
41%

International:
3%

Out-of-State:
11%

Political Activity

Campus is very politically active, and more liberal than conservative. Many on-campus groups are social and political activism organizations.

Gay Pride

LGBT Center and clubs are very active and visible on campus.

Most Popular Religions

Christian, Muslim, spiritual but not religious. (A large percentage of students also consider themselves agnostic or atheist.)

Economic Status

Varied; mostly middle and middle-upper class.

Minority Clubs

There is high visibility and participation of minority organizations at Cal. The most active on Sproul Plaza are Asian organizations, minority business organizations, Christian and other religious groups, and ethnic volunteer organizations.

Students Speak Out On...
Diversity

> "I would say that the diversity of the campus is, overall, not bad. I think blacks and Hispanics are a little underrepresented, though."

Q "Our campus is one of the most diverse in the country. There are so many different types of people, and I think that's great. You end up learning so much about so many different cultures—it makes you a well-rounded person. Berkeley's extremely diversified campus is one of the reasons that it's the best in the country. You'll find yourself sitting around with a group of friends at two in the morning, having stimulating conversations about different issues in the world . . . these are my favorite times. **Learning off campus can be a big part of your experiences**."

Q "We have students that feel very strongly about everything. Whenever a conflict occurs internationally, or you see a controversy on the news, we have at least two student groups out on our main plaza protesting or handing out information about their cause. It's really exciting to be on a campus where **young people have such strong convictions about their world**."

Q "As a black female, **I feel like Berkeley is not as diverse as it claims to be**. There's a substantially smaller percentage of black and Hispanics admitted to Berkeley compared to the general population, making it hard for the minorities on campus to fully integrate into the larger academic society."

Q "**The diversity at Berkeley is the source of a lot of student tension**, but also a lot of intellectual stimulation, too. The arguments on campus about affirmative action, conflict in the Middle East, religion, politics, women's rights—all of these daily battles are what makes Berkeley such a unique, and sometimes aggravating, place to go to school."

Q "I haven't met two people with the exact same views, and I rarely come across people who don't have any opinions on at least one important issue. **People are generally knowledgeable and interested in politics and international issues** because they come from all around the world and often have experienced or seen first-hand the things they are arguing about. I don't know any other university in the U.S. that could provide such an enriching student environment."

Q "Honestly, the first year I was a student at Berkeley, I was really impressed, and even excited, by the constant on-campus arguments over politics, social issues, and that sort of thing. But by my sophomore year, either I became really jaded, or **I just realized how pointless a lot of the stuff that was going on was**. The same people were touting their same ideologies, over and over to their dogmatic opponents, who weren't ever going to change their minds. I began thinking that the diversity here didn't really expand people's minds, it just identified more enemies for people to fight."

Q "One generalization people have about Berkeley is that students are really self-righteous, and I have to say that for the most part, I think it's true. We give ourselves certain entitlement because we live in a really liberal place and we think we're supposed to be politically conscious, have a cause, and be totally politically correct. **For the most part, no one really knows what they're talking about**, and a lot of vocal people are just BS-ing."

Q "Diversity? Hmm, it exists, but only in certain areas. Political diversity? Not really. I'd say 90 percent of the people in Berkeley are liberal if not ultra-liberal, and the remaining 10 percent are either apathetic or conservative. But this doesn't include the huge percentage of people who are secretly one way but publicly another. Berkeley is supposed to be a really tolerant place, full of different cultures and different views, but there's one vein of thought that runs through the majority of people's minds, and I've noticed that **the people who claim to be the most liberal and compassionate** are sometimes the most intolerant and prejudiced."

Q "Diversity is probably the first word that comes to mind when I think of Berkeley. The characters on the street, in your classes, running your classes, making your coffee, fixing your refrigerators—everyone in Berkeley comes from a different background, has a different perspective on the world, and knows something that you don't. All of my friends and I have agreed that **we've learned the most outside of the classroom**, discussing ideas and politics with friends, professors, strangers . . . learning new things through experiencing the real world, not by reading a textbook."

The College Prowler Take On...
Diversity

Campus diversity, along with a long list of other hotly-contested issues, is a big deal at Berkeley and sparks both criticism and praise. A not-so-small number of people found Berkeley's campus diversity to be a myth rather than a reality, and a surprising amount share the belief that Berkeley is more homogeneous than commonly assumed by outsiders, especially compared to other UCs and public schools. A handful of students said that the racial diversity was not all-encompassing enough, and even if it were, the socioeconomic and background diversity would still be lacking.

Despite these views, other Berkeley students and faculty see the school's population as undeniably diverse. Differences in race, ethnicity, age, background, and religious and political views are what make Berkeley fresh and invigorating. These students think that those who believe Berkeley to be monotonous have been living in the bubble too long. Regardless, there's perhaps few other places that can foster such contrasting ideas and opinions with so much openness, and in such a dense, academic environment.

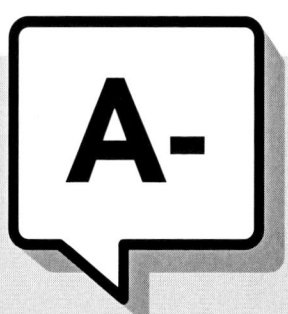

The College Prowler® Grade on
Diversity: A-

A high grade in Diversity indicates that ethnic minorities and international students have a notable presence on campus and that students of different economic backgrounds, religious beliefs, and sexual preferences are well-represented.

Guys & Girls

The Lowdown On...
Guys & Girls

Men Undergrads:
46%

Women Undergrads:
54%

Birth Control Available?
Yes, covered by University Health Insurance, available at the Tang Center

Most Prevalent STDs on Campus
HPV, oral herpes, genital herpes

Percentage of Students with an STD
12–20 percent

Did You Know?

Top Places to Hook Up:
1. Lawrence Hall of Science
2. Tilden Park
3. Greek Theatre
4. In a frat bathroom
5. In the back of the Pacific Film Archive movie theater

Social Scene
Urban college town with a hip hop/alt-Indie/electronic music scene

Hookups or Relationships?
Hookups are most prevalent; serious relationships and casual relationships are not as common.

Best Places to Meet Guys/Girls
International House

Café Strada

Recreational Sports Facility

Strawberry Canyon Pool

San Francisco bars and parks

Students Speak Out On...
Guys & Girls

> "If you're only looking for blonde bimbos, male or female, go to UCLA, UCSB, or USC. Berkeley isn't for you."

 "**The stereotypical Berkeley guy or girl is 'granola**,' laid-back, and pretty smart. Granola pretty much means earthy, environmentally conscious, etc. Notice how there's no mention of physical attractiveness. Yeah, Berkeley students aren't known for being hotties, but that's probably because the majority of people focus on less superficial things than just their looks—like their work, their education, and personal goals and interests. There are definitely some made-up, pretty girls around campus, so if you're into that, then don't worry. But for the most part, people are down-to-earth and into relationships."

"A lot of the people I've met here aren't necessarily attractive in the conventional sense, but they are still self-conscious and style-conscious in that alternative-Indie, or outdoorsy kind of way. For a lot of people, that's a lot better than just run-of-the-mill attractiveness, but to me, I think it's all the same. **Berkeley has a lot of righteous people who are really cool, smart, and informed**, but who also have to express their identities through every facet of their lives—even down to their shoe brands and environmentally-friendly detergents."

"I'd like to meet someone to spend quality time with, go on trips with, talk to . . . but I really don't have the time. With school, research, work, and basketball, **there's no time for a social life** besides going out on weekends with friends."

Q "**There's always talk of the lack of hot girls and guys at Berkeley**, but I've definitely come across a lot of not only good-looking, but actually interesting, nice people here, especially in class and through Greek life. I come from Southern California, and there's definitely a different type of hotness that dominates there, but I think some of the girls I've met here are not only naturally good-looking, but intelligent and cool."

Q "Guys at Berkeley are very nice. It's nice to meet guys who care about their future and are considerate. We have our good share of hot guys, but I guess it's a matter of taste. I've always managed to find a hot guy in the crowd, but of course **we do have our share of dorky boys, too**. The girls at Cal are also very nice. I've made so many great friends this year, and I think that's because Berkeley attracts quality people; it's a very diverse campus."

Q "Berkeley admits the elite of our country, so the majority of people are more interested in acquiring knowledge and studying. Of course, since we're young, we're also interested in dating. Just remember that hardly anyone comes to Berkeley solely to pursue the opposite sex! Having said that, there are around 20,000 undergrads at Berkeley; I'm sure you can find a guy or girl that's good-looking enough for you. **I don't think there's a shortage of hot girls**; it's just a matter of whether or not I have the time to pursue them, and whether or not they're attracted to me. But then again, looks aren't everything. A lot of Berkeley girls are attractive because they're down-to-earth, fun to hang out with, and still really hard-working and smart."

Q "There are tons of beautiful men at Berkeley, but unfortunately, **they're either gay or taken**."

Q "The people at Berkeley are definitely different. It's a shock coming to Berkeley for people who come from a small town. I'm not from a small town, but I was totally shocked to see people out in the grassy areas just toking away at their bong and no one bothering them. It depends on what kind of guy or girl you like, but there's someone for everyone; **sometimes you just have to look**."

Q "**Lots of guys joke about 'Cal-vision'** because all the women are so ugly, they start looking good. I've heard girls say the guys aren't much better, but I've read somewhere that it's like third in the country for eligible guys; that was like four years ago. Anyways, there are plenty of attractive people if you look hard enough."

Q "**The guys and girls at Cal all seem to have one thing in common: they're ambitious**. Whether they're working their asses off for their sports team, a good GPA, grad school, or a weekend partying, everyone understands that hard work is necessary to get by here. That said, I think that most of the students at Cal are catches because they have the right attitude and, usually, good intentions."

Q "I've been dating my high school boyfriend since I started going to Berkeley until now, and I haven't felt the desire to break up with him because I haven't really met anyone here that seems worth my time. **It's really hard to approach people here** because all the guys are either shy, or look like they're arrogant. Finding friends is pretty hard, but finding boyfriends or girlfriends is almost impossible."

Q "There are always some skeezeballs that hit on all the girls at the local bars, like Blake's and Kip's, but even if they're cool, they come off as gross because so few people see open flirtation as acceptable. Finding love or even casual dating at Berkeley is hard, so most people go to the bars and clubs in the city, where **people are less uptight and more down for whatever**."

The College Prowler Take On...
Guys & Girls

Berkeley has never really prided itself on its "hot" guys and girls, maybe for good reason. Though some conventionally and exotically attractive men and women can be spotted on campus everyday, most Berkeley students choose to focus on their activities, schoolwork, and friends, rather than their appearances or clothing. Many male students complain about the small proportion of physically attractive female students at Berkeley. For the most part, female students exert very little effort into their appearances, and it definitely shows. The girls, however, are not without their complaints about the guys at Berkeley. Many complain that the guys at Berkeley are either too shy or uninterested in the opposite sex to initiate conversation that could lead to a possible date. Due to these factors, the dating scene is barely existent.

Although the opposite sex at Berkeley may not offer much from the dating perspective, both sexes speak highly of the opposite sex as friends, conversationalists, and activity partners. Many of the students have interesting opinions and beliefs and, for the most part, seem to be down-to-earth. The guys and girls at Berkeley appear to have their heads on their shoulders and respect each other for their intelligence, activity in the community, and high level of motivation.

The College Prowler® Grade on
Guys: B

A high grade for Guys indicates that the male population on campus is attractive, smart, friendly, and engaging, and that the school has a decent ratio of guys to girls.

The College Prowler® Grade on
Girls: C

A high grade for Girls not only implies that the women on campus are attractive, smart, friendly, and engaging, but also that there is a fair ratio of girls to guys.

Athletics

The Lowdown On...
Athletics

Athletic Division:
Division I-A

Conference:
PAC 10

School Mascot:
Oski the Golden Bear

Men Playing Varsity Sports:
506 (5%)

Women Playing Varsity Sports:
371 (3%)

Men's Varsity Sports:
Baseball
Basketball
Cross-Country
Crew
Football
Golf
Gymnastics
Rugby
Soccer
Swimming
Tennis
Track & Field
Water Polo

Women's Varsity Sports:
Basketball
Cross-Country
Crew
Field Hockey
Golf
Gymnastics
Lacrosse
Soccer
Softball
Swimming
Tennis
Track & Field
Volleyball
Water Polo

Intramurals:
Basketball
Flag Football
Soccer (Indoor)
Softball
Speed Soccer
Ultimate Frisbee
Volleyball

Club Sports:
Badminton
Ballroom Dance
Boxing
Lightweight Crew
Cycling
Fencing
Gymnastics
Handball
Field Hockey (Men's)
Ice Hockey
Lacrosse (Men's)
Racquetball
Rugby (Women's)
Sailing
Soccer
Squash
Tennis
Triathalon
Ultimate Frisbee
Volleyball (Men's)

Athletic Fields

6 tennis courts surrounding campus

Edwards Stadium (track and field) surrounding the Goldman Field (soccer)

Evans Diamond (baseball)

Field House in RSF (volleyball)

Golden Bear Pool

Haas Pavilion (basketball, gymnastics)

Hearst Gymnasium and Pool

Levine-Fricke Field (softball)

Maxwell Family Field (field hockey)

Memorial Stadium (football, lacrosse)

Recreational Sports Facility (RSF)

Strawberry Canyon Fitness Center and Pool

Whitter Rugby field (rugby)

Getting Tickets

Online at *http://calbears.ocsn.com/tickets/cal-tickets.html*

Or at the Cal Athletic Ticket Office:

2223 Fulton St. 1st Floor

Berkeley, CA 94720-4422

1-800-GO-BEARS

Open: Monday–Friday, 8:30 a.m.–4:30 p.m.

Tickets cannot be bought online for Cal away games.

Most Popular Sports

Basketball

Crew (Men's)

Football

Rugby

Water Polo (Men's)

Overlooked Teams
Gymnastics (Men's)
Softball
Tennis (Women's)

Best Place to Take a Walk
Fire Trails behind Strawberry Canyon
Marin Headlands
Tilden Park

Gyms/Facilities
Cal Rec Club
The Rec Club contains five swimming pools, two running tracks, a well-equipped weight room, racquetball, handball, squash, tennis, and basketball courts, and two outdoor fields for soccer, softball, and other field activities.

Recreational Sports Facility
The RSF has an olympic-sized swimming pool, three gyms for volleyball, badminton or indoor soccer, seven full size basketball courts, six squash courts and seven racquetball/handball courts. Activity classes offered include aerobics, BOSU ball, studio cycling, kickboxing, step aerobics, dance, pilates, strength training, yoga, and many more!

Outdoor Tennis Courts
Six tennis courts are available by reservation in one-hour time blocks.

Students Speak Out On...
Athletics

> "Our football team had a huge turnaround a few years back and is getting stronger, so I've heard. Cal games have always been awesome and fun, but with even better sports teams, they should be even cooler."

Q "Even though Berkeley is supposed to be a bunch of bookworms, there are still some first-rate athletes that go to this school, and people know it. **There are always Cal fans at the basketball games and football games**, and even at some of the less popular sports events. Cal students like to be well-rounded, and athletics is no exception."

Q "Football season is huge. Home games are Saturday afternoons, and on game days, everyone gets up at 10 a.m. and starts partying around 11 a.m. All the students wear blue and gold, and the fraternities have open barbeques and bars in their front yards (you walk down Greek row to get to the football stadium). So basically, it's just one big street full of Cal fans eating hot dogs and drinking beer and margaritas. **We also have a rally committee that leads the whole student section in cheers during games**; it's lots of fun. Even if our football team is doing badly, people can tell when they don't hear the Cal victory cannon, and just stay at the game-day parties."

Q "Berkeley has lots of school spirit . . . and lots of spirit means that varsity sports are very big on campus. Our football team isn't the best, but you still have a great time at the game, win or lose. **Our pride for Cal is incredible**. Our basketball team is awesome! The games are lots of fun. IM sports are also big, and they're easy to join."

Q "**Sports aren't big on campus**. People like to have fun and occasionally go to games, but, overall, a lot of people don't pay attention."

Q "If you make an effort to get involved, **you'll never run out of things to do**. You'll actually find yourself having to ration out your time because there are so many club sports teams, PE classes, and other things going on."

Q "**Football games are the best ever**! All I've got to say is that it's always a big game when Stanford and Cal play. It's amazing. The rivalry is great. Having great sports makes the students really involved. IM sports are pretty big here, too. We also have club sports, which are more competitive than IM sports."

Q "I loved playing IM soccer my freshman year. I wasn't on the soccer team in high school, but I always liked messing around. So when a couple of friends and I got together to form a team when I lived in CKC, I finally got to play competitively. **I found out that I was actually darn good**! I had a lot of fun playing against awesome players, who obviously did play in high school but just wanted to play to have a good time in college."

Q "I had nothing against Stanford until they held up a sign saying 'you will work for us' at the first 'big game' I went to; we've been rivals for like 100 years or so, and it gets really competitive in a couple of sports. **A few years back, our rugby team had been national champions for, like, 12 years**; they even forfeited to us one year because they didn't want to get hurt."

Q "Varsity sports are very big on campus. IM sports are very popular among many students, and the 'Golden Bear Axe Game' is always very talked about because our rivalry with Stanford is such a tradition. Of course, you know we have a very good basketball team, good representatives to the Olympics, and we also have a hockey team—basically all major college-level sports teams we have. **Any sport available anywhere in the U.S. is one we most likely have** and are also pretty good at."

The College Prowler Take On...
Athletics

Berkeley's reputation as an academic school doesn't hinder its competitive athletic performance in several sports, most notably basketball, rugby, gymnastics, and football. Cal's heavy recruitment of athletes from around the world helps booster both sports scores and student body diversity. Though one of Cal's top sports, rugby, isn't one that is talked about too frequently, many of the other teams are at the most competitive levels in the country and have gained the attention of both Cal and non-Cal fans. Students are proud of Cal's sports teams, even when they aren't on top, and celebrate the many nationally-ranked athletes that attend or have graduated from Cal. School spirit is either very high or very low, depending on whom you ask. The majority of students say that Cal has as much spirit as any other large university, but there are a few students who point to Cal's diversity as separating students and making it hard for one unified school spirit to be felt.

Cal's very active intramural sports competitions are also fun for recreational play, as well as the Cal Adventures program that trains students in kayaking, sailing, rock climbing, snorkeling, and other less conventional sporting activities. Cal STAR is another school-sponsored program that matches physically disabled students and adults with student volunteer trainers.

The College Prowler® Grade on
Athletics: B

A high grade in Athletics indicates that students have school spirit, that sports programs are respected, that games are well-attended, and that intramurals are a prominent part of student life.

Nightlife

The Lowdown On...
Nightlife

Club and Bar Prowler: Popular Nightlife Spots!

Club Crawler:

The club scene is not prominent in Berkeley; most people head to Oakland or San Francisco for clubbing or dancing.

Ashkenaz Music and Dance Center

1317 San Pablo Ave.

(510) 525-5054

www.ashkenaz.com

Ashkenaz is a popular dance club and show venue, featuring music and artists of Balkan, Blues, Cajun/Zydeco, Middle Eastern, African, Caribbean, and Reggae persuasion. Ashkenaz is family/child friendly.

City Nights
715 Harrison St.
(415) 339-8686
www.sfclubs.com

An 18-and-over San Francisco club, City Nights is one of the few clubbing options. The club generally plays hip hop, Top 40, and dance music, and is only open Saturdays, 9:30 p.m. until 2:30 a.m.

Shattuck Downlow
2284 Shattuck Ave.
(510) 548-1159

Shattuck Downlow is probably the only real club in Berkeley; every night has a particular theme ranging from salsa, to karaoke, to hip hop. Most patrons are older and not UCB students. The bar and club are actually pretty swank, with plush couches and subtle lighting, but the Downlow has yet to escape its cheesy reputation.

Bar Prowler:

Due to the lack of other nightlife options in the immediate area, Berkeley students often find themselves at the same

(Bar Prowler, continued)
handful of local bars. Though many complain that the Berkeley bar scene is predictable and overwrought with drunken frat boys, it's still the most convenient and affordable place to party.

The Bear's Lair Pub
2475 Bancroft Way
(510) 843-5247

The Bear's Lair attracts a wide variety of students with its cheap drink specials and event nights. On most weekend nights, you'll find athletes, Greek scenesters, and groups of students and adults just hanging out.

Blakes on Telegraph
2367 Telegraph Ave.
(510) 848-0886

Attempting at a little more style than the other bars, Blakes is a tri-level bar and dance club that has drinks on the second and third levels and live music in the basement. The clientele is diverse, ranging from Berkeley townies to underage lushes.

Henry's Publick House & Grille
2600 Durant Ave.
(510) 845-8981

Henry's attracts an older crowd on most nights, but at around 9 p.m. on Tuesdays, it transforms into a sweaty, crowded meat market. Their infamous "Two for Tuesdays" drink specials aren't so special once you take a look at the size of their cocktails, but it's still fun to think you've drank six long islands instead of three.

Kip's
2439 Durant Ave.
(510) 848-4340

The favorite for late-night (if you can call 1:30 a.m. late night) drinkers, Kip's is where everyone ends up when all the other bars close. Drinks are cheap, girls look cheaper, and everyone is having a good, drunk ole time.

Raleigh's
2438 Telegraph Ave.
(510) 848-8652

Most people will say that Raleigh's has the least obnoxious and most laid-back scene out of all the bars, but it closes at midnight (sorry night owls).

Other Places to Check Out:

In San Francisco

The Mission District (bars, food), North Beach (bars, strip clubs), Haight Street (bars, live music), Folsom St. (bars, clubs), and the Castro District (bars, clubs)

In Oakland

The Ruby Room (bar), Radio (bar), the Alley (piano bar), Oasis (dance club/bar)

Useful Resources for Nightlife:

Diablo Magazine

San Francisco Magazine

SF Weekly (free)

www.sfstation.com

www.sfbg.com

www.bestofberkeley.com

www.mecurynews.com

Cheapest Places to Get a Drink:

Daily dirt-cheap pitchers at Raleigh's

Two cocktails for the price of one, Tuesdays at Henry's

Daily cocktail specials at Blakes

Local Specialties:

Bison Brewery hard iced tea kegs

Student Favorites:

The Bear's Lair Pub, Blakes, Henry's, Kip's, and Raleigh's

Bars Close At:

12:30 a.m.–2 a.m.

Primary Areas with Nightlife:

Broadway, College Avenue, Durant Avenue, Telegraph Avenue, San Pablo Avenue, and Shattuck Avenue

What to Do if You're Not 21

Concerts at 924 Gilman (music venue)

Shows at Ashkenaz Music and Dance Center

Piedmont Spa (Jacuzzis, saunas in Oakland)

18-and-over nights at Blakes or City Nights

Organization Parties

Residence Hall Dance Parties, Residence Hall End-of-the-Year Boat Party, ASUC Winter Ball, UCB-sponsored movie/preview nights at Wheeler Auditorium

Frats

See the Greek section!

Students Speak Out On...
Nightlife

> "Blakes actually has some pretty cool live bands downstairs, but not that many people know about that. The upstairs floors of the bar are cool—cheap drinks and filled with pretty good-looking girls."

Q "Berkeley bars are pretty fun if you're just looking to get snookered and walk around for most of the night. They used to be a lot easier on fake IDs, but because a lot of the bars got in trouble for letting underage students in, they've gotten a lot stricter. **I got rejected from Kip's once because I had a fake—it sucked**. Raleigh's is probably the strictest because they got publicly charged, and there was a huge scandal about drunk, underage girls being served in the bar."

Q "**City Nights is the club that all the freshman have to go to** because it's not 21 and over. For a club, it sucks—it's dirty and cramped. For a freshman, it's the only thing you've got."

Q "Blakes, Kip's, Raleigh's, and especially the Bear's Lair, are filled with frat boys and sorority girls who are only interested in getting to know only each other. There's the occasional Berkeley townie that tries to hit on all the young college girls, but **no one really pays attention to the non-Berkeley students**. I'd say get out of Berkeley if you want real night life, but just for a casual beer, the bars around here are fine."

Q "**Berkeley nightlife is nonexistent**. There are no good dance clubs, the bars are filled with the same boring people every night, and there are rarely any good parties that don't get broken up way early. Some people like how exclusive it is, like a college town, but I think it gets boring."

Q "For bars and clubs, I would say that the places to go are Blakes and Kip's. These seem to be the main bars close to campus. I'm not much of a drinker, and I'm not of age, so I don't go too often. Blakes features live music and DJs each night. Also, the International House isn't a bad place to hang out if you're underage. As far as clubs are concerned, it depends on what you like. **I haven't seen any good dance clubs around**, but I prefer dancing in warehouses anyway, so that's okay. If you like reggae, there's a pretty good club called Ashkenaz. If you're into punk, there's Gilman."

Q "The mission district in SF has been infiltrated with really bourgeois art kids and boring yuppies that go to all the cheap taquerias and bars on the weekend. It's kind of hip, but now that everyone goes, it's lost its appeal. If you're into just straight up, filthy boozing, go to North Beach, the sleaziest part of San Francisco. **There are tons of drunk guys walking around, going to bars and strip clubs, harassing girls**. It's hilarious. There's some pretty good food, too."

Q "**You gotta go Greek if you want to party in Berkeley**. Honestly, I've only been to one or two good house parties here. The rest of the fun times I've had in this neighborhood have all been at frats, or were frat-organized events."

Q "Buy a San Francisco guidebook. There are so many neat places to just hang out, party, drink, dance, and do anything in the city, that you'll want a book to make sure you cover everything. **My favorite place to go at night is the Castro District**. I'm a girl, and I like that I don't get totally groped when I dance because most of the people dancing are gay men!"

Q "**The bar scene is relatively strong; the club scene is nonexistent**. Go to San Francisco or Oakland for that kind of stuff. The party scene more than compensates; you just have to meet some people in the Greek system, which is not difficult."

Q "I don't really go to clubs much. I'm so tired of that scene. There are frat parties, but I heard they aren't all that. But you can always take the F bus or the BART to San Francisco's clubs. By the way, city buses are free for students since we have that AC transit pass. **The F bus takes you to San Francisco for free**!"

Q "We have a pub on campus, the Bear's Lair. There are a few bars in downtown Berkeley, but **most people go to either fraternity parties or San Francisco to get really wasted**."

The College Prowler Take On...
Nightlife

Berkeley's nightlife is quaint. There are the few popular bars that almost always promise the same lot of people every night. Then there are the few choice bars, farther off the path, that Berkeley kids who are sick of the tired local scene often escape to. But according to the majority of students interviewed, being involved in the Greek scene is the easiest and most surefire way to have a rocking social life, though an awesome night out is entirely possible if you aren't in a sorority or a fraternity.

If you're not going Greek, and you're tired of the same bar-goers you see every night at Kip's and Blakes, then your best bet is to head on over to the most romantic (and arguably, hip) city in the U.S.—San Francisco. Anything that you could want to do—have a nice dinner, watch an indie movie, go to a rave, get crazy at a strip club, get nasty on the dance floor, just grab a beer with your friends—you'll find a perfect place to do it in some nook of the city. In some ways, you have the best of both worlds—you have the convenience of college town dives to zip into and grab a cheap drink, yet you also have the glitz and glam of city bars and clubs at your fingertips, at a $15–$30 cost.

The College Prowler® Grade on
Nightlife: B-

A high grade in Nightlife indicates that there are many bars and clubs in the area that are easily accessible and affordable. Other determining factors include the number of options for the under-21 crowd and the prevalence of house parties.

Greek Life

The Lowdown On...
Greek Life

Number of Fraternities:
39

Number of Sororities:
19

Undergrad Men in Fraternities:
10%

Undergrad Women in Sororities:
10%

Fraternities on Campus:

Acacia
Alpha Chi Sigma
Alpha Epsilon Pi
Alpha Gamma Omega
Alpha Kappa Delta
Alpha Kappa Psi
Alpha Phi Alpha
Alpha Sigma Phi
Alpha Tau Omega
Alpha Xi Omega
Beta Theta Pi
Chi Phi
Chi Psi
Delta Chi
Delta Kappa Epsilon
Delta Tau Delta
Delta Upsilon
Kappa Delta Rho
Kappa Sigma
Lambda Chi Alpha
Lambda Phi Epsilon
Phi Beta Sigma
Phi Delta Theta
Phi Gamma Delta
Phi Kappa Tau
Pi Alpha Phi
Pi Kappa Alpha
Pi Kappa Phi
Pi Lambda Phi
Sigma Alpha Epsilon
Sigma Alpha Mu
Sigma Chi
Sigma Nu
Sigma Phi Epsilon
Sigma Pi
Theta Delta Chi
Theta Xi
Zeta Beta Tau
Zeta Psi

Sororities on Campus:

Alpha Beta Zeta
Alpha Chi Omega
Alpha Delta Chi
Alpha Delta Pi
Alpha Kappa Alpha
Alpha Kappa Delta Phi
Alpha Omicron Pi
Alpha Phi
Chi Omega
Delta Delta Delta
Delta Gamma
Delta Sigma Theta
Gamma Phi Beta
Kappa Alpha Theta
Kappa Kappa Gamma
Pi Beta Phi
Sigma Kappa

Other Greek Organizations:

Interfraterninty Council
Multicultural Greek Council
National Panhellenic Council

Students Speak Out On...
Greek Life

> **"The sororities and fraternities here aren't hardcore like at many other schools. We don't wear our letters to class, nor do we hang out exclusively with members of our house or the Greek community."**

Q "Greek life at Cal is a very interesting phenomenon. Berkeley is one of the most laid-back schools anywhere; there are so many different types of kids, and everyone is very accepting of everyone else. Greek life at most colleges tends to be more gung-ho, but at Berkeley, **the Greek scene reflects the same general laid-back atmosphere**, which is really nice."

Q "**Berkeley has a big Greek system, but it doesn't dominate the social scene**. I decided not to join a sorority, and I still attend frat parties. They really don't care if you are not part of the system. Greek life in Berkeley is good; they hold good parties, and you get to meet nice people. You absolutely do not have to join in the system in order to join in on the fun."

Q "Greek life is pretty big on campus. I don't have much interest in it, but there's a pretty big Greek scene. Personally, **I find their parties and lifestyle to be lame**, but that's just me, I suppose."

Q "**There are quite a few Greek chapters at Berkeley**, although recently, the University banned alcohol from all Greek parties and events. Whether or not it dominates the social scene depends on which group you tend to hang out with. For me, since I'm engineering major, it wasn't at all a factor. Your social life in college totally depends on what you make out of it. Nobody's going to monitor who you hang out with or what you do, so it's all up to you."

Q "Greek life does not dominate the social scene, but frat parties are really cool to go to, if that's your thing. **I enjoy my fraternity and the parties they throw**. Social life is what you make of it. If you want it to be involved in Greek life, you can, but it's not the only thing going on."

Q "I am involved in the Greek system. The Greek scene does not rule the campus, yet it can be considered the main social scene because there are also a lot of people who never leave their room and just study, study, study. But since Berkeley is so diverse, the Greek scene isn't always dominant. Other people could care less about the Greek scene. **I like it because Berkeley is so big; it gives me something to associate with**. You can easily get lost here, but by associating with different clubs on campus or the Greek system, it usually makes things a little easier."

Q "Greeks are low in number but manage to dominate the social scene. **They are the only social scene**. The rest of the school tends to keep it to the books, hence the academic reputation. If you intend on working and playing hard, Greek life is going to be your only opportunity to do so."

Q "**I believe only a small percent of Cal students are in the Greek system**, so there are other things to do around campus. Clubs and cultural groups hold a ton of events, and there's always some event going on in Berkeley or San Francisco. There are cheap movies shown on campus and lots of stuff to do every day."

Q "Our Greek system is pretty small, but the people in it think they own Berkeley's entire social scene. In some ways, they do because there are so few cool places to hang out in Berkeley, but students definitely branch out of the area and go to San Francisco so that they don't have to only engage in the Greek community. If you want to just stay in Berkeley for most of your time and hang out with the same people pretty much 24/7, then look into rushing. If not, **you've got a lot of other options.**"

Q "**Frat guys and sorority girls definitely have a stigma attached to them at Berkeley**. There's a stereotypical Berkeley frat-guy and sorority-girl look. Berkeley frat guys are usually white, unless it's a special race-specific frat. They're rich, wear Abercrombie & Fitch and flip-flops, and eat Cheese 'n Stuff sandwiches. They're usually jerks, too. Sorority girls are white, rich, wear Abercrombie & Fitch and flip-flops, eat Yogurt Park, and they're usually fake or stuck-up. But maybe these are stereotypes that are true at all schools. Berkeley is definitely aware of them, though, and a lot of people have come to think they're true."

Q "**The best party I've been to my three years at Cal was the Blacklite party at the Kappa Sigma house**. Everyone was wearing white under these black lights, and they got fluorescent paint thrown all over them! People were crammed in there, all drunk, high, whatever, and dancing. By the end of the night, I was covered in alcohol, paint, and other people's sweat. I'll never forget that night."

Q "**Greek is weak**, but it's a good way to fix your housing problem and give yourself a quick and easy social life. It's a convenient way to make sure you have food, DSL, friends, and housing in one full swoop, and ins to the biggest parties on campus of the year."

The College Prowler Take On...
Greek Life

Greek life at Berkeley is prominent but not dominant. People in fraternities and sororities range from being totally immersed in their Greek social lives, to feeling somewhat apathetic towards the Greek scene. While fraternities put on some of the largest and most well-funded parties, there's typically a guest list or bid system, so you must be friends with an organizer to ensure entrance. However, most sorority girls and fraternity boys at Berkeley cite reasons beyond just partying privileges for going Greek, like gaining a sense of closeness in a house and in a community, having easy access to Greek-only parties, events, and other social benefits, and making connections for jobs and internships through chapter alumni.

But while there are definite amenities attached to being in the Greek scene, there are also undeniable drawbacks. Parties are fun in the beginning, but the redundancy and the bar scene usually lead students to become disinterested by their sophomore years. UC Berkley has also recently put its second alcohol ban on Greek events in the past several years. Though this clearly doesn't stop Greeks from partying, it certainly puts a damper on their fun, at least for a short time. Many of the people that were not part of the Greek scene said that they either had seriously considered it at one point, or had actually joined and de-pledged. The consensus among these people was that while being in a fraternity or sorority was fun and convenient in many ways, it became too socially constricting and superficial.

The College Prowler® Grade on
Greek Life: B+

A high grade in Greek Life indicates that sororities and fraternities are not only present, but also active on campus. Other determining factors include the variety of houses available and the respect the Greek community receives from the rest of the campus.

Drug Scene

The Lowdown On...
Drug Scene

Most Prevalent Drugs on Campus:
Adderall
Ecstasy
Hallucinogens
Marijuana
Methamphetamines

Liquor-Related Referrals:
319

Liquor-Related Arrests:
43

Drug-Related Referrals:
90

Drug-Related Arrests:
110

Drug Counseling Programs:
Tang Center's Alcohol and Drug Counseling
(510) 642-6074

Students Speak Out On...
Drug Scene

"It's out there—I've seen it. There's a lot of weed and a lot of coke. Students also now use Adderall to study here. Be prepared for weed world. There are way too many people who smoke weed."

Q "I personally have never seen students abusing drugs. I've heard of some people who smoke pot, but it's definitely not the Berkeley of the '60s. We're more mature, generally more conservative and goal-oriented, and 'cleaner.' **I'm sure that many students do drugs in their rooms or with their friends**, but it's pretty well-hidden."

Q "I think that **Berkeley really doesn't have a big drug scene**. I think the one drug that you would say that's pretty prominent on campus is pot, but people are not going to pressure you to do anything you don't want to do. In any situation, you have the decision to say yes or no. The drug scene on campus isn't scary."

Q "**Well, it's Berkeley**; you can get just about anything here, but people are pretty private about drug use."

Q "If you want drugs, you can find them, and if you don't, you can avoid them. Berkeley's famous **Telegraph Avenue is not quite the drug center it was 20 years ago**, but they're still out there."

Q "**Pot is fairly common**. I know a few people who've done hallucinogens, and the co-ops have lots of drugs. I did nothing; I didn't even drink."

Q "Well, as far as the drug scene on campus, it's there if you want it, and not there if you don't. There's a lot of diversity at Berkeley. I would say weed is the drug of choice among the campus. A lot of people smoke, and it's pretty easy to get it. Berkeley has a reputation for its embrace of counterculture, so it's not surprising that you can find most any drug, if you so wish. **Next to weed, I'd say 'shrooms are the next commonly used drug**. I'm sure you can find a myriad of psychedelics. But if you don't like drugs, don't feel threatened. Most people don't do drugs here, but I know a lot who do."

Q "Resident advisors are pretty strict about drug use in the dorms; they don't give a lot of leniency to people who are caught drinking or smoking weed. **I know a couple of people who've actually smoked with their RAs, but that's rare**."

Q "Pot is prevalent. It's chill, though. **Some of the smartest and best students I know are pot users**. But of course there are those potheads that are part-time students who just sit around playing video games and stuff. Don't become like that; it's a waste of your education."

Q "**I'd say there are more drug users at Cal than at most universities**. That's probably because some of the people who come to Berkeley associate the school and the city with its hippie past and want to come here and relive it or something."

The College Prowler Take On...
Drug Scene

Students agree that drug use is far from nonexistent at Berkeley and is even seen as part of popular campus culture by many. Most people name pot and psychedelics as the most frequently-used drugs, while harder drugs like cocaine, methamphetamine, and ecstasy are less-frequently used. The latest trend has been students using prescription drugs, such as Adderall and Ritalin, to do school work or party all night. Berkeley is a liberal place, and its liberalness often comes with a blind eye towards most drug use.

Though Berkeley is a very different community than it used to be in the sixties and seventies, it still has remnants of its past that can be seen in its persistently prominent drug culture. The pervasiveness of pot and psychedelics, as well as harder narcotics, is a substantial concern for Berkeley residents and police. Pot is, by far, the most popular drug, and law enforcement has become almost permissive with its private and public use. Of course, drug busts are frequent and should not be taken lightly. Still, it is pretty much expected that Berkeley students will experiment, hopefully safely, while they're here and not run into much trouble doing so. But an overwhelming number of drug-users and non-drug-users agree that substance abuse is the surest way to fall behind as a student.

The College Prowler® Grade on
Drug Scene: C

A high grade in the Drug Scene indicates that drugs are not a noticeable part of campus life; drug use is not visible, and no pressure to use them seems to exist.

Campus Strictness

The Lowdown On...
Campus Strictness

What Are You Most Likely to Get Caught Doing on Campus?
- Riding your bike in pedestrian-only areas
- Cheating
- Stealing
- Consuming alcohol
- Smoking marijuana

Students Speak Out On...
Campus Strictness

"From what I've seen, the school is pretty lax. It's like a 'don't ask, don't tell' policy. In the dorms, though, you can get in trouble if your resident advisor finds out."

Q "Campus police are pretty cool about drinking, but you still have to be careful. Drugs are against the law, and **if cops find you doing some, then you'll probably get in lots of trouble**."

Q "Everyone complains about campus police because they can be tightwads about walking your bike, wearing your helmet, etc. But really, they're pretty relaxed compared to other campuses I've been to. A friend of mine got taken to the precincts when he went to Pomona because he was drunk on school property. **The only time I deal with the UCPD is when I'm at a party and it's getting too loud** and out of control, and it's understandable why they have to come and break it up."

Q "**Campus police can be jerks sometimes**. The only cool thing about the police force in Berkeley is that they're very lenient on weed. I smoke all the time on campus with no troubles. They mostly leave students alone and deal with everyone else on and near campus."

Q "Drinking in the dorms is a major bust. If you're loud, which you probably will be, you'll get caught by your RA and written up. It's a hassle. **Go to a bar or a house if you want to drink**."

Q "**It's pretty strict if you live in campus housing**, but if you want to drink or do drugs once you move out, it's open. Just don't be dumb about it and do it on campus. Walk two blocks off of campus."

Q "They have their moments when they're strict about it. Frats have been getting in trouble recently. **On game days, they don't care at all, and they look the other way**. There are plenty of drugs here, but I think that's true about every college campus."

Q "The city of Berkeley passed a law prohibiting its own police force from helping the DEA in marijuana-related drug investigations, and it seems like **everybody knows somebody who can get him or her a fake ID**. Getting into bars and drinking without one is pretty tough, but it's still possible."

Q "**Police usually only respond to complaints (noise, crowds, etc.)**. If it doesn't get out of hand, they usually leave well enough alone."

Q "It's not very strict; I haven't heard of any major crackdowns. My friend **smoked pot while walking down the street** because he figured he wouldn't get in trouble; I think that's a bit extreme—I think you could get busted for that."

The College Prowler Take On...
Campus Strictness

Students at Berkeley have pretty good things to say about campus police and security, citing few incidents of unreasonableness or unjust treatment. But police are police, and blatant misconduct will land you in academic and legal trouble. While living in the dorms, you'll most likely run into more trouble with your resident advisor than any other campus officer, so it's important to stay on good terms with him or her. Stealing and cheating are the two most frequent on-campus infringements and are dealt with primarily by campus security, while drug use, theft, and assault are the biggest crimes in the city of Berkeley and are handled by the police.

Berkeley is known for having somewhat lenient law enforcement when it comes to marijuana use, underage drinking, and drinking in public, but there are always the rare cases where police have to crack down, and a first-time offender can get in severe trouble. There are more prominent risks for students (muggings, street violence, etc.), and police don't spend as much time on the smaller crimes that college students are prone to committing. Students are pretty happy with campus police because most officers understand that they're dealing with college students and leave room for them to make some mistakes.

The College Prowler® Grade on
Campus Strictness: B

A high Campus Strictness grade implies an overall lenient atmosphere; police and RAs are fairly tolerant, and the administration's rules are flexible.

Parking

The Lowdown On...
Parking

Parking Permit Cost:
$140 per year

Berkeley Parking Services:
UC Berkeley Parking & Transportation
http://public-safety.berkeley.edu/p&t

Freshmen Allowed to Park?
Yes, but an extremely limited number of permits are issued.

Student Parking Lot?
Yes

Common Parking Tickets:
Expired Meter: $29
No Parking Zone: $34
Fire Lane: $39
Handicapped Zone: $39

Parking Permits

School Permits – Difficult to get; must have physical disability or live outside certain designated area.

City Permits – Must show two proofs of residency in Berkeley, and car must be registered in Berkeley.

Did You Know?

Best Places to Find a Parking Spot
Below Telegraph, towards Shattuck; the farther south of campus, the better.

Good Luck Getting a Parking Spot Here
Anywhere within two blocks of campus, especially Bancroft, Durant Avenue, and Channing.

Students Speak Out On...
Parking

"Parking is a nightmare. If you go to this school, expect to walk around town a lot. In fact, cars are only useful if you want to get out of Berkeley."

Q "Don't even think about bringing a car. You don't want one unless you have an apartment with an assigned parking space. Parking is impossible to find. Most of my friends with cars have ten or more parking tickets. Besides, you don't want a car. **There's a lot of public transportation available.** All students get a free bus pass, which will get you all around Berkeley. BART is a subway that goes to San Francisco, and it's easy to use."

Q "**Parking is a big issue in Berkeley**. Having a car is not a good idea; you really don't need one."

Q "Parking is horrible in Berkeley, so I wouldn't bring a car, if possible. **The city of Berkeley is very anal about the congestion that they claim the University causes**, and the two often fight over proposed expansions of student housing or parking facilities."

Q "**Do not bring a car**. It isn't needed. You have one of the best public transportation systems in the United States. Parking is hard unless you live far from campus."

Q "For your budget's sake, for your health's sake, for the environment's sake—**don't bring a car**."

Q "Don't bring a car your freshman year. Not only is parking hard, but the car is not necessary. We have great public transportation—BART and the bus. Plus, there's easy access to airports. And, **most likely, one of your friends will have a car**."

Q "Parking is terrible. But, most places are within walking distance. The city of Berkeley issues a limited number of parking permits per year, just to park on the street. Yep, **you can get a ticket just for parking on the street**."

Q "A car is a giant headache. **Parking fees are outrageous, and lots are overcrowded**. Luckily, Berkeley is very dense and has a great public transportation system. A car is far from necessary."

Q "I have a car here, even though it can be a hassle. **I like having access to an easy escape from Berkeley**. I give a lot of my friends rides to the city, and they're glad that I have a car."

Q "If you're from Southern California, you're probably used to driving to get somewhere three blocks from your house, so a car might feel like a necessity. You will really get used to not having one after a couple of years, but some people can't wait that long and just bring one up because, even though parking is expensive, **it's a lot more convenient than catching the bus or walking**."

Q "Yeah, there are a lot of crazy people on the bus, and it's almost always packed, but trust me, I had a car up here for a semester, and **the trouble of riding the bus is nothing compared to the trouble of parking**, paying tickets, getting permits, and giving your friends rides around town."

The College Prowler Take On...
Parking

Parking tickets, traffic, and likely insurance spikes are all reasons to leave your car at home and not bring it to school (especially for your first year at Cal). Berkeley is not a car-friendly place, with pointless roadblocks, random one-way streets, and confusing parking restrictions near campus and in residential areas. The majority of students say that bringing a car to school is a bad idea, money-wise and sanity-wise. Students say that public transportation is convenient, relatively cheap, and widespread, so getting to places (even San Francisco and Oakland) is usually quick and easy. Obtaining school parking permits, as well as city permits, is a hassle, and they are not guaranteed to all who apply.

While there are more reasons to forget about your car than to bring it, a small number of students say that their experiences at Berkeley have actually improved after bringing their cars to school. Students are always excited when their friends bring their cars because that means shopping, traveling, and running errands can be done faster and simpler, and more of the Bay Area is open to them. And if you do decide to bring it, make sure that you've got enough money in the bank—you'll definitely need to draw on your emergency cash for the first five tickets you'll get from parking on street sweeping days or being two minutes late on filling your meter.

The College Prowler® Grade on
Parking: D

A high grade in this section indicates that parking is both available and affordable, and that parking enforcement isn't overly severe.

Transportation

The Lowdown On...
Transportation

Ways to Get Around Town:

On Campus
UCB daytime and night safety shuttles
Day shuttles run from 7:40 a.m. to 7:30 p.m.
Night shuttles run from 7 p.m. to 6 a.m.
(510) 642-5149
http://public-safety.berkeley. edu/p%26t/transit/index.html

Public Transportation
Bay Area Rapid Transit (BART)
Runs from 5 a.m. to 12 a.m.
www.bart.gov

AC Transit
Runs 24 hours a day
www.actransit.org

Taxi Cabs
A Cab
 (510) 548-8000
Berkeley Yellow Cab
(510) 548-2561 or
(510) 548-2233

(Taxi Cabs, continued)
Grand Lake Taxi
(510) 540-6282

Khalsa Taxi SVC
(510) 649-8200

Local & Airport Cab Co.
(510) 841-8294

Yellow A-1
(510) 845-3333

Yellow AA Cab
(510) 486-0400

Car Rentals

Avis
local: (510) 548-7363
national: (800) 831-2847
www.avis.com

Budget,
local: (510) 486-0806
national: (800) 527-0700
www.budget.com

Enterprise
local: (510) 526-3900
national: (800) 736-8222
www.enterprise.com

Hertz
local: (510) 562-7888
national: (800) 654-3131
www.hertz.com

National
local: (510) 549-1580
national: (800) 227-7368
www.nationalcar.com

City Carshare
(415) 995-8588
www.citycarshare.org

Best Ways to Get Around Town

AC Transit, bicycle, moped/motorcycle, walk

Ways to Get Out of Town:

Airlines Serving Oakland and San Francisco

American Airlines,
(800) 433-7300
www.americanairlines.com

Continental, (800) 523-3273
www.continental.com

Delta, (800) 221-1212,
www.delta-air.com

Northwest, (800) 225-2525,
www.nwa.com

Southwest, (800) 435-9792,
www.southwest.com

United, (800) 241-6522,
www.united.com

Airports

Oakland International Airport (OAK)

(510) 563-3300

www.oaklandairport.com

About a 20-minute drive; 1 hour BART/bus ride from Berkeley.

San Francisco International Airport (SFO)

(650) 821-8211

www.sfoairport.com

About a 45-minute drive, 1 hour, 40-minute BART/bus ride from Berkeley.

How to Get to the Airports

The easiest way to get to or from the Oakland and San Francisco (SFO) airports is to take a shuttle van, which is like a taxi, but much cheaper.

(How to Get to the Airports, continued)

Fares run from $15-$19. When taking a shuttle, be sure to call the company ahead of time to make a reservation and to confirm departure times.

BayPorter Express shuttles pick you up at your doorstep and run to both OAK and SFO (www.bayporter.com; $19 one-way or $32 round-trip; (877) 467-1800).

City Express Shuttle serves Oakland and San Francisco and offer student discounts.

Luxor services the Oakland airport ($15 with student discount, 7 a.m.– 10 p.m.).

A cab ride to Oakland International costs $30-$40; to San Francisco International, $60-$70.

BART to Airports

Using BART and transferring to a local bus is the cheapest and easiest option, if you don't have a lot to carry.

Oakland Airport by BART: catch the Richmond-Fremont line in the Fremont direction and get off at Coliseum. Take an Air-BART shuttle to the Oakland Airport (these leave every 15 minutes and cost $2). Buy your ticket in the station before boarding the bus (runs Monday–Saturday, 6 a.m.–11:50 p.m.; Sunday, 8:30 a.m.–11:50 p.m.).

(BART to airports, continued)

You can also take AC Transit bus #58 from the Coliseum BART to the airport (runs daily, every 20-30 minutes from
5 a.m.–12 a.m. and hourly, 12 a.m.–5 a.m.).

SFO by BART: an extension has just been constructed to take you directly to SFO via BART. Get on the Daly City train at the Downtown Berkeley station, transfer at Balboa Park onto the SFO train. One-way costs about $6.

Greyhound

2103 San Pablo Ave.
Oakland CA 94612
(510) 834-3213

Amtrak

(Un-staffed) Amtrak Station
3rd St. and University Ave.
Berkeley, CA 94710
(800) USA-RAIL

Caltrain

Provides commuters travel between SF and Gilroy, via San Jose: (800) 660-4287

Travel Agents

STA Travel, 2410 Telegraph Ave., Berkeley, (510) 644-0772

Budget Travel, 2387 Telegraph Ave., Berkeley, (510) 848-8604

Students Speak Out On...
Transportation

> "We have one of the best public transportation systems in the United States. We have BART, which is like the subway, and the AC Transit bus system, which goes everywhere except Stanford."

Q "Public Transportation is very convenient and popular. On your ID card, you will get an AC Transit pass sticker, which allows you to use any bus or shuttle in Berkeley and Oakland. **You just show the sticker and walk right in**; it saves you from all of the trouble of looking for spare change."

Q "**Public transportation is very convenient**. With tuition, you get a bus pass for AC Transit, which runs mostly in the East Bay. There is also a Transbay bus, the F, to San Francisco. The pass is placed on your student ID. BART is close as well, giving you access to much of the Bay Area."

Q "BART fees are rising, but it's still a good deal—you can go anywhere in the city, SFO airport even, within an hour. **The AC Transit is really extensive** in the Berkeley area, and with your pass, you can get all your errands done pretty easily."

Q "I never took the bus when I went to UCLA, but now that I'm at Berkeley and the city bus system is so accessible, I think it's actually easier than driving around everywhere. I think the Bay Area is one of those places that is the **most exciting when it's walked through at your leisure, unlike LA**."

Q "I use public transit everyday. It's not bad at all, and **BART takes you almost anywhere you need it to**."

Q "It's great and takes me everywhere since I don't have a car! BART is **not as efficient as the NY subway**, but it works."

Q "BART station is a five-minute walk from campus and a fifteen-minute walk from the dorms. **Busing is also really good**."

Q "I use the campus day and night shuttles everyday. I have classes on the farthest ends of campus, so **the 15-minute perimeter shuttles make it really easy to get from class to class**, and from class to work. The best part is that all the shuttles are free for Berkeley students."

Q "Bikes are definitely the transportation mode of choice. There are so many cyclists in the Bay Area because it's a beautiful terrain, and it's so much easier to get around by bike than by car. **There are a lot of bike trails around the city** and in Berkeley, and there is almost always a bike lane to ride safely with other traffic."

The College Prowler Take On...
Transportation

Most students are satisfied with, and fully utilize, the Berkeley public transportation systems. They say that it's definitely a better alternative to bringing a car, and that the extra time expended is minimal and easy to adjust to. BART is an 80-mile-per-hour rail system that connects many points, at seven to fifteen minute service times from 5 a.m. to midnight within the Bay Area. It takes about twenty minutes to get from downtown Berkeley to San Francisco, and it costs less than three dollars. The Downtown Berkeley station is about a ten-minute walk or a short shuttle or bus ride from main campus.

Berkeley knows that its students must have easy and accessible ways to get around town, so they've set up extensive public transportation systems that diminish the need for personal vehicles. Bicycle and pedestrian-friendly, Berkeley has set up extremely helpful shuttle and bus services that make frequent stops, run as late as 3 a.m., and are usually free of charge. Berkeley has successfully made using public transportation, and being nice to the environment, more of a convenience than a pain.

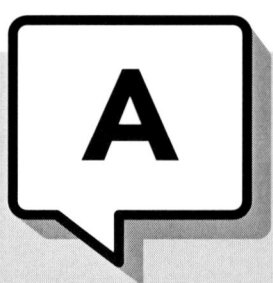

The College Prowler® Grade on
Transportation: A

A high grade for Transportation indicates that campus buses, public buses, cabs, and rental cars are readily–available and affordable. Other determining factors include proximity to an airport and the necessity of transportation.

Weather

The Lowdown On...
Weather

Average Temperature:
Fall: 60°F
Winter: 50°F
Spring: 56°F
Summer: 64°F

Average Precipitation:
Fall: 4.44 in.
Winter: 13.0 in.
Spring: 5.59 in.
Summer: 0.28 in.

Students Speak Out On...
Weather

> "I live in a place where it's basically hot all the time. Coming to Berkeley was a big change, but it wasn't bad. I mean, it gets cold, it gets rainy, and it gets sunny. The weather was never a big issue for me."

Q "The Bay Area has pretty mild whether all year long. **It never really gets hot; it never snows**."

Q "The rain sucks! I'm from Southern California, so I was expecting the weather to be a little bit more like it is down there. I **was really surprised when I spent my first winter here and it would rain for weeks straight**."

Q "The weather is pretty nice. It's **moderate most of the time**, with a cool breeze from the ocean. During the winter, it can get quite cold and rainy, but overall, it's not too bad. It gets foggy in the summer."

Q "Berkeley has probably the best weather in the entire United States. We get mild conditions all year round. Summers are cool and dry, with highs usually in the 70s and low 80s. **We get morning and evening fog**, which acts as natural air-conditioning and keeps the air fresh and cool. Spring and fall are usually clear and warm as well, while winter is when we get most of our rain. Lows in the winter are probably in the 40s, with rain on maybe thirty to forty percent of the days. Overall, it's the best weather you could ask for."

Q "**The air seems really fresh up here**. Berkeley is near real, unadulterated nature—it's just a really healthy-feeling sort of climate."

Q "Some people think it gets really cold during the winter, and they don't want to leave their dorms or their houses. But **I'm from the East Coast, and I think it's actually kind of nice**. It's definitely not as cold as it gets over there, so I have nothing to complain about."

Q "It's somewhat mild; **we don't have extremes in the winter or in the summer**. The temperature doesn't go much below the 50s in the winter and above the 80s in the summer."

Q "**It never gets really hot or really cold**. It's not nearly as humid as the East. My ideal outfit is jeans, short sleeve shirt or tank top, and sandals. I usually take a fleece because it can get cold. At night when I got out, I usually wear pants."

Q "In August and September, **it is quite warm, but it quickly becomes cold and rainy**. Buy a warm coat and a good umbrella."

Q "Weather is one of the most complained-about things at Berkeley, especially by Southern Californian kids. It can be a real downer. **I know a lot of people who get kind of depressed every time the fog and rain roll in**, but if you go about it the right way, you can actually start to think it's nice and refreshing."

Q "It's kind of cool, people get really excited when there's a nice day in Berkeley because it doesn't happen all that often, and usually when it's nice, it's really nice. **The weather is totally made for outdoor activities** like running, hiking, swimming, sailing, and sometimes even surfing, though the ocean is super cold."

The College Prowler Take On...
Weather

Generally, students don't have a lot to really gripe about when it comes to Berkeley weather. The climate in the Bay Area tends to be pretty mild, aside from the occasional rainstorm and heat wave. An umbrella and good boots/rain shoes are must-haves, as well as tank tops, flip-flops, and sunglasses. The rainy weather has the potential to depress some students, but most get used to it and actually begin to look forward to the occasional cozy afternoon inside.

Hot, cold, humid, dry—Berkeley weather runs the gamut, but usually in moderation. It's no Southern California, but it is still California nonetheless, and more often than not, Berkeley residents have little reason to stay cooped up inside. Also, the relative lack of smog and proximity to the mountains, trees, and ocean make Berkeley's air much cleaner and clearer than what most people are used to. Berkeley's mild climate and varied topography are two of its arguable advantages over other universities in the country, especially the often frigid East Coast, and even in California.

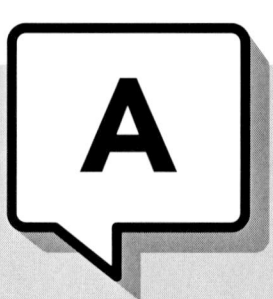

The College Prowler® Grade on Weather: A

A high Weather grade designates that temperatures are mild and rarely reach extremes, that the campus tends to be sunny rather than rainy, and that weather is fairly consistent rather than unpredictable.

UC BERKELEY
Report Card Summary

A- ACADEMICS	**B** GUYS
B+ LOCAL ATMOSPHERE	**C** GIRLS
B- SAFETY & SECURITY	**B** ATHLETICS
B+ COMPUTERS	**B-** NIGHTLIFE
B+ FACILITIES	**B+** GREEK LIFE
C CAMPUS DINING	**C** DRUG SCENE
A OFF-CAMPUS DINING	**B** CAMPUS STRICTNESS
B CAMPUS HOUSING	**D** PARKING
C OFF-CAMPUS HOUSING	**A** TRANSPORTATION
A- DIVERSITY	**A** WEATHER

Overall Experience

Students Speak Out On...
Overall Experience

> "I've never been happier in my life than where I am now, here in Berkeley. Both the campus and town are amazingly diverse and offer opportunities for just about everything."

Q "At first, I had a hard time adjusting to the 'hippie-ness' of the area. I thought I had made the wrong choice. But by October, I had made a lot of great friends, loved my classes, and had joined some campus organizations—I was **having the time of my life**. Berkeley is such a great school; the classes really make you think and work hard, and in some cases, they have really inspired me. The people you meet here are amazing; I'd never want to go anywhere else."

Q "Overall, my time here has been awesome. **I've had such a fun and rewarding experience**. I came to Berkeley without ever visiting, and I have never regretted my decision. I definitely do not wish that I went somewhere else. I love Berkeley, and I can guarantee that you won't find any other place like it. Berkeley is a very distinguished school; its history is amazing, and the people are one-of-a-kind. You will not find better quality people anywhere else."

Q "**I loved my four years at Berkeley**. They were very challenging, and I never studied harder in my life, but it was worth it. I love the people I met through classes and campus groups and will probably keep in touch with many of them for a long time. Given the amount of education and benefits, Berkeley is the best deal out there."

Q "Although it has been really tough for me, I wouldn't want to be in another school. **Berkeley is one of the toughest and most competitive schools in the country**, and those two qualities allow Berkeley to prepare its graduates better than any other school."

Q "It's the best place for me. I absolutely love this school. I love the history behind it; I love watching the news and seeing my school on TV; I love seeing the sporting events. **I have met some amazing people here** from all backgrounds. It's a large campus, which I wanted. Another way for me to describe Berkeley is by comparing it to when you watch movies and see the 'perfect college experience'—I feel like I am living that."

Q "I love Cal because we have some of the best faculty in the world, so the professors are great. The campus is beautiful. You'll meet interesting people if you try really hard to make friends, but **I hate it because classes are huge**—between 300 and 400 people—so most of the time you're just a face in the crowd. No one really cares about undergraduates here, and you're treated pretty badly."

Q "If I could do it over again, I would go to a smaller, private school. I hated my freshman year here; **I was miserable and almost moved back home**."

Q "Maybe I've had a bad experience, but undergrads at a research university with 32,000 students are **not cared for at all as individuals by faculty**."

Q "Overall, my experience at Berkeley was pretty good. **I just wish I would've been more involved in activities** and gotten more out of school."

Q "**I already graduated, but I can truly say that I really, really enjoyed my years at Berkeley**. It was the best time of my life—but most people say that their college experience was great. I was considering going to UCLA instead of Berkeley, but I'm so glad that I decided to go to Cal instead. I love it there, and I drive one and a half hours almost every weekend to visit."

Q "It was really hard for me to adjust when I first got here. I'm from Orange County, CA, so the atmosphere was definitely very different from what I was used to. Even though making friends, dealing with small inconveniences, and talking to professors were all kind of tough, I think **the challenge made me stronger and more equipped for the real world**."

Q "There are a lot of little annoyances about Berkeley that you can either let get to you, or you can just let go of. Berkeley is not for everyone. **It's not for people who don't want a challenge**. It's not for people who doubt themselves too much. And it's not for people who can't stand a little rain and cold weather."

Q "**Berkeley offers the most bang for your buck**. A first-rate education at a fraction of the price you'd pay to go to a small private school, so many interesting folks around, and San Francisco a half hour away—there's not a lot more that you could want."

Q "When you take everything into consideration, **the problems with Berkeley don't outweigh the benefits it offers**. There are so many things to do, for fun and in school; there are so many types of people and professors to meet and work with. There really is an opportunity for you to do anything you want. But you really have to find things you want, focus on them, and go after them, or else you can easily let awesome opportunities slip through your fingers."

The College Prowler Take On...
Overall Experience

Overall, students have very positive things to say about their experiences at Cal, stating that there is no other place they could have met the extraordinary people, professors, opportunities, and challenges. But Berkeley is known for being home to some insatiable critics, and some who give it a relatively good grade still cite annoyances you must come to expect and endure if you want to make the most of your time at Berkeley. The bureaucratic nuisances of waiting in long, seemingly pointless lines and being known as a number, rather than a person, combined with the little sympathy you receive from teachers or other students for poor performance or attitude are elements of Cal that several students gripe. Some eventually get over them.

The most annoying things about Berkeley—its sometimes over-impacted classes, icy professors, cut-throat competitiveness, and occasional sense of social confinement—are all part of being at a public school with a large, diversified student body. Some people will argue the extra $40,000 a year you pay to attend a small, private school goes into smoothing out these problems, and that the money spent is well worth it. However, the majority of Berkeley students go through, at times, the exhausting process of acclimating and growing to love their large university, asserting that they've gained more academic strength, tenacity, and open-mindedness than they could have at any other institution. They even have an extra hundred grand or so in their pockets!

The Inside Scoop

The Lowdown On...
The Inside Scoop

UC Berkeley Slang:

Know the slang, know the school. The following is a list of things you really need to know before coming to UC Berkeley. The more of these words you know, the better off you'll be.

The City – San Francisco.
CKC – Clark Kerr Campus.
DC – Dining commons.
Down the Hill – The bars near Telegraph (Henry's, Blakes, and Kip's).
FSM – Free Speech Movement Café.
GBC – Golden Bear Café.
Ghetto Food Court, Food Ghetto – Asian food court on Durant Ave., between Telegraph and Bowditch.

Invitational – A dance party students must be invited to, usually organized by sororities or fraternities; typically involves free transportation, alcohol, and free entry to a dance club.

Stacks – Gardner Main Stacks (popular library study spot).

Tight – Cool, great, perfect. ("That move you did on the dance floor was tight.")

Trashed, wasted, hammered, sloshed, obliterated, messed up – Drunk, high, or combination thereof.

Whack – Unfair, unfortunate, usually used in describing a minor injustice. ("The way your boyfriend broke up with you was whack.")

Things I Wish I Knew Before Coming to UC Berkeley

- How cold it gets in the winter.
- Professors care less about you than you do about them.
- Get to know your professors for recommendations later.
- IKEA is just ten minutes away.
- Finding an affordable apartment is a year-long commitment.
- How big some classes are.
- Get on a small meal plan.

Tips to Succeed at UC Berkeley

- Don't develop a drug/alcohol habit.
- Do as many extracurricular activities as you can handle.
- Go abroad if you can.
- Don't be discouraged by the smart, ambitious, and hard-working renaissance men and women around you.
- Don't give up your academic dreams.
- Go to class.

UC Berkeley Urban Legends

- Two students committed suicide by jumping off the top floors in Evans Hall one year, leaving it with a curse.

- A parking lot was built exclusively for Nobel Laureates.

- The brownies at the Dining Commons are laced with marijuana.

- Sather Gate could fall down in the event of a major earthquake.

Traditions

Oski
This is the official mascot of UC Berkeley. This big, friendly golden bear wears a college letterman's sweater and is often seen at athletic games and other special events on campus. He's an undercover party animal and can be seen pouring and downing beers at the Bear's Lair Brewpub from time to time.

Cal vs. Stanford Football Game, a.k.a. "The Big Game"
This is the pinnacle of our sports year. The axe is the prize for the victor of this monumental annual game pitting the Cal football team against its cross-town rival, Stanford. The antagonism between Cal and Stanford has gone on for a century and continues to be one of the strongest signs of our school spirit to this day. Stanford is the most despised school among Cal fans, and the Big Game during football season is one of the only times we get to show them just how nasty we can get. The stadium, Stanford's or Cal's depending on the year, is always packed with students, family, and alumni—ranging from the class of 1956, to current students—sporting shirts, hats, and flags of gold, blue, and crimson. And be careful—don't get caught wearing red (Stanford's color) the week of the Big Game, or you might get pointed out on campus, told by roaming Rally Committee members and athletes to "take off that red," and hassled until you do.

Football Pre and After-Parties on Frat Row
The frats start drinking before noon on football game days, and they usually continue the festivities deep into the night with live music, dancing, and free alcohol. You can find at least one frat having a huge post-game party, and you'll most definitely find lots of drunk Greek scenesters roaming the local bars on those nights, too.

Homecoming and Parent Weekend
This is within the first few months of school and is usually when the Cal parents and alumni show up to either relive their college years or just check in with their kids. There are games, food, events, lectures, exhibits, tours, and lots of people all over campus who are all smiles for Cal. It's a good time to remind yourself of how lucky you are to be a Berkeley student.

SUPERB Spring Concert Series
These are noon concerts held on Lower Sproul every Friday that usually feature small or Indie/alternative bands. Bigger name bands such as Homegrown and Mates of State have been featured before, but the biggest crowd pleasers are usually booked for the free, end-of-the-year concert at the Greek Theater. Tickets run out quickly, so make sure you get yours early. Previous year's performers included Jurassic 5, Living Legends, Norah Jones, the Pixies, and the Roots.

Finding a Job or Internship

The Lowdown On...
Finding a Job or Internship

You can ask an employer in any field, and there's a good chance he or she knows of UC Berkeley and is familiar with its prestige as a top-notch university. But that by no means guarantees you a job anywhere, unless you have an equally impressive resume, history, and list of reliable references. Having a Berkeley degree will win you major points with employers in fields ranging from electrical engineering to anthropology, but it will not make up for a poor academic record, bad references, or no related experience. Spend your time wisely and be active. Conducting research for professors, volunteering or interning, and participating in student organizations are just a number of ways to gain experience and build your resume.

Advice

Start early and work hard—it's that simple. Look for open positions in the Undergraduate Research Apprenticeships Program (URAP) every semester to see if you can help out a professor's work-in-progress and make a valuable connection with him/her as a mentor and reference. Try to do internships or volunteer, even if they are unpaid, because it is often in those positions that you receive the most hands-on training for the fields you are interested in. If you need spending money and the job is non-paid, see if you can handle a part-time job at a café or restaurant, along with a more serious internship or apprenticeship.

Career Center Resources & Services

UC Berkeley Career Center
http://career.berkeley.edu
2111 Bancroft Way
Berkeley, CA 94720-4350
Phone: (510) 642-1716
Fax: (510) 643-6120

Undergraduate Research Apprenticeship Program:
http://research.berkeley.edu/urap

Average Salary Information

Berkeley graduates have been known to do almost anything post-graduation, from traveling around the world as a Hari Krishna for a few years before heading to business school, to becoming an expatriate in South America and opening up a successful dance club. The range of salaries that students receive depends on many variables—whether or not they are in graduate/professional school, whether they live abroad, and whether they are seriously looking for employment or just testing the waters.

Average starting salaries for just-finished undergraduates:

Haas School of Business	$54,900
School of Chemistry	$45,000
School of Engineering	$55,000
School of Environmental Design	$33,700
School of Natural Resources	$39,000
School of Letters and Sciences	$32,000

Alumni

The Lowdown On...
Alumni

Web Site:
www.alumni.berkeley.edu

The California Alumni Association (CAA):
The Alumni House
Berkeley, CA 94720-7520
Toll-Free: (888) CAL-ALUM
Phone: (510) 642-7026
Fax: (510) 642-6252

The Alumni House:
The Alumni House is situated in a quiet nook of campus and consists of the Toll Room, a 120-300 person occupancy room that is used for conferences, lectures, receptions, and workshops and is often rented out for banquets and special events. The Stephen Bechtel Conference Room, the President's Room, and the President's Conference Room are used for conferences and class gatherings.

Services Available:

Job listings exclusively for Cal alums, career workshops, the Alumni Networking Program, Lair of the Golden Bear Mountain Summer Camp, regional, ethnic, and special interest alumni clubs, *California Monthly* magazine, CAA Alumni Awards, access to renting Alumni House facilities.

Major Alumni Events

Homecoming

This is probably the most fun and exciting event for proud Cal alums who are just itching to relive their college years, or at least remember them. During this activities-packed weekend, alums visit Cal to join in on the football frenzy and booze and schmooze with their old professors and/or their sons and daughters while reuniting with students in their classes and student organizations. There are several lectures, shows, parties, and banquets the weekend of Homecoming—some open to the public and others restricted to Cal alums only.

Lair of the Golden Bear Summer Camp

Every summer, Cal alums from all over the world come together at Stanislaus National Forest in California to partake in the fun and relaxing alumni retreat known as the Lair. Camping, hiking, swimming, and other camp activities integrate Cal alumni and their family with generations of Oski-lovers, both old and young.

Alumni Publications

California Monthly

Since its establishment in 1905, this bi-monthly magazine has now racked up a mailing list of 85,000 Cal alumni and has received twelve outstanding journalism/photojournalism awards within the last fifteen years. The magazine consists of current events, Cal-related news, and news surrounding Cal alumni.

Did You Know?

Famous Berkeley Alumni

Jonathan Kenneth Galbraith (class of 1932) – Famous economist and advisor to President Kennedy.

Walter Haas (class of 1910) – President of Levi Strauss & Co., for whom the Haas School of Business is named.

Julie Morgan (class of 1894) – Architect of the Hearst Castle.

Gregory Peck (class of 1939) – American actor in such films as *Roman Holiday* and *To Kill a Mockingbird*.

Nicklaus Wirth (class of 1963) – Developer of Pascal and Modula-2 programming languages.

Steve Wozniak (class of 1986) – Co-founder of the Apple Computer.

Student Organizations

There are over 730 Office of Student Life-approved organizations on the Berkeley campus, with new groups receiving charters every semester. If you have a specific interest that you share with other students on campus, from fencing to physics, there's most likely a group for you. If not, you can start one with enough time and effort. Visit *http://uga.berkeley.edu/sas/student/groupsearch.asp* for a list of approved groups.

The Best & Worst

The Ten **BEST** Things About UC Berkeley

1	Huge, diverse, and intellectually-driven student body
2	World-renowned and inspiring faculty
3	Large and abundant academic and athletic facilities
4	Proximity to San Francisco's cultures and communities
5	Natural amenities (marinas, parks, trails, ocean, etc.)
6	DECAL program to start your own class
7	Academic prestige in professional circles
8	A plethora of good dining options right off campus
9	Thought-provoking and world-famous speakers
10	Prevalence and convenience of public transportation

The Ten WORST Things About UC Berkeley

1	Local street squatters (homeless people)
2	High academic pressure
3	Abundance of choices often hinders decision-making
4	An overly-accepted drug culture
5	Rainy weather in the winter
6	Lack of local hot spots as opposed to San Francisco
7	A college-town feel that can, at times, feel suffocating
8	Lack of parking and the non-car-friendly UC policies
9	The work-related pretentiousness of some students
10	Some frigid and inaccessible professors and GSIs

Visiting

The Lowdown On...
Visiting

Hotel Information:

Bancroft Hotel
2680 Bancroft Way, Berkeley
(510) 549-1000, (800) 549-1002
www.bancrofthotel.com
22 rooms
Newly restored,1928 national historic landmark; smallish rooms; right across the street from campus.
Distance from Campus: Less than 1 mile
Price Range: $100–$200

Bay Bridge Holiday Inn
1800 Powell St., Emeryville
(510) 658-9300
www.ichotelsgroup.com/h/d/hi/1/en/hd/sfoob
279 rooms
Distance from Campus: 3 miles
Price Range: $110–$190

Berkeley City Club
2315 Durant Ave., Berkeley
(510) 848-7800
www.berkeleycityclubcom
40 rooms
National historic landmark

(Berkeley City Club, continued)

designed by Julia Morgan; includes lap pool and parking.

Distance from Campus: Less than 1 mile

Price Range: $110–$130

Berkeley Marina Radisson

200 Marina Blvd., Berkeley

(800) 243-0625

www.radisson.com/home.jsp

375 rooms, 80 with marina views

On the water; health club, two pools, boat dock, restaurant.

Distance from Campus: 3 miles

Price Range: $105–$225

Concord Hilton, Concord Station

1970 Diamond Blvd., Concord

(800) 445-8667

www.hilton.com/en/hi/hotels/index.jhtml?ctyhocn=CONCHHF

294 rooms

Distance from Campus: 18 miles

Price Range: $166–$200

Faculty Club

UC Berkeley

(510) 642-1993

http://berkeleyfacultyclub.com

23 rooms

Comfy, historic clubhouse, partly designed by Bernard Maybeck, in picturesque Faculty Glade.

(Faculty Club, continued)

Distance from Campus: On Campus

Price Range: $53–$210

Four Points Hotel—Sheraton

1603 Powell St., Emeryville

(510) 547-7888, (800) 325-3535

www.sheraton.com

153 rooms

Bay Area views

Distance from Campus: 3 miles

Price Range: $89–$219

French Hotel

1538 Shattuck Ave., Berkeley

(510) 548-9930

18 rooms

In the heart of the North Shattuck shopping/dining area.

Distance from Campus: Less than 1 mile

Price Range: $90–$149

Holiday Inn, Walnut Creek

2730 North Main St., Walnut Creek

(800) 924-6835

www.ichotelsgroup.com/h/d/6c/1/en/hd/wcrca

155 rooms

Distance from Campus: 14 miles

Price Range: $100–$180

Hotel Durant
2600 Durant Ave., Berkeley
(800) 238-7268
www.hoteldurant.com
140 rooms
Built in 1928, a Berkeley institution with popular pub.
Distance from Campus: Less than 1 mile
Price Range: $130–$219

Hotel Shattuck Plaza
2086 Allston Way, Berkeley
(510) 845-7300
www.hotelshattuckplaza.com
143 rooms
Old-fashioned; very convenient location.
Distance from Campus: Less than 1 mile
Price Range: $106–$186

Oakland Marriott, 12th Street Station
1001 Broadway, Oakland
(800) 288-9290
http://marriott.com/default.mi
79 rooms
Distance from Campus: 5 miles
Price Range: $175–$255

Pleasant Hill Embassy Suites
1345 Treat Blvd., Walnut Creek
(800) 362-2779
www.embassysuites.com/en/es/hotels/index.jhtml?ctyhocn=SFOPHES
249 suites
Distance from Campus: 14 miles
Price Range: $130–$260

Walnut Creek Marriott, Walnut Creek Station
2355 North Main, Walnut Creek
(800) 228-9290
http://marriott.com/default.mi
338 rooms
Distance from Campus: 13 miles
Price Range: $109–$200

Woodfin Suite Hotel
5800 Shellmound St., Emeryville
(888) 433-9042
www.woodfinsuitehotels.com/emeryville
Distance from Campus: 3 miles
Price Range: $140–$180

Take a Campus Virtual Tour

www.berkeley.edu/tour

To Schedule a Group Information Session or Interview

There are no interviews conducted for prospective students. To schedule a group information session or tour, call (510) 642-5215 from 9 a.m.–4 p.m.

Campus Tours

Free 90-minute campus tours are held daily, seven days a week. Trained student guides who are knowledgeable about the Berkeley campus and student life at Cal lead these walking tours. You do not need to make a reservation if your party is fewer than ten people.

Tours begin at 10 a.m., Monday through Friday, and depart from the Visitor Center at 101 University Hall, located at the corner of University Avenue and Oxford Street. These Monday through Friday tours are also followed by a 30-minute admissions presentation for prospective freshmen who have not yet applied to the University. Saturday and Sunday tours begin from the Campanile in the center of campus; Saturday tours begin at 10 a.m.; Sunday tours begin at 1 p.m.

Directions to Campus

From Northbound Highway 101 (San Francisco/Daly City)
- Follow Highway 101 North, then take I-80 East/Bay Bridge.
- Once across the bridge, stay to the left. Exit at University Avenue, and continue east for approximately two miles to the campus.

From Westbound or Eastbound I-80
- Exit at University Avenue, and continue east for approximately two miles to the campus.

From Westbound Highway 13
- Highway 13 becomes Tunnel Road as it enters Berkeley, and then changes to Ashby Avenue near the Claremont Hotel.
- Turn right onto College Avenue, which will take you to the campus.

From Westbound Highway 24
- Travel through the Caldecott Tunnel, and take the Telegraph Avenue Exit.
- Turn right onto Telegraph, and continue north for approximately two miles to the campus.

From Northbound I-880 (San Jose, Hayward, Oakland International Airport)
- Follow I-880 East. Stay in left center lanes for I-80 East (to Berkeley).
- Take the University Avenue exit, and continue east for approximately two miles to campus.

From Westbound I-580
- Exit I-80 East (to Berkeley, Sacramento).
- Take the University Avenue Exit, and continue east for approximately two miles to campus.

Words to Know

Academic Probation – A suspension imposed on a student if he or she fails to keep up with the school's minimum academic requirements. Those unable to improve their grades after receiving this warning can face dismissal.

Beer Pong/Beirut – A drinking game involving cups of beer arranged in a pyramid shape on each side of a table. The goal is to get a ping pong ball into one of the opponent's cups by throwing the ball or hitting it with a paddle. If the ball lands in a cup, the opponent is required to drink the beer.

Bid – An invitation from a fraternity or sorority to 'pledge' (join) that specific house.

Blue-Light Phone – Brightly-colored phone posts with a blue light bulb on top. These phones exist for security purposes and are located at various outside locations around most campuses. In an emergency, a student can pick up one of these phones (free of charge) to connect with campus police or a security escort.

Campus Police – Police who are specifically assigned to a given institution. Campus police are typically not regular city officers; they are employed by the university in a full-time capacity.

Club Sports – A level of sports that falls somewhere between varsity and intramural. If a student is unable to commit to a varsity team but has a lot of passion for athletics, a club sport could be a better, less intense option. Even less demanding, intramural (IM) sports often involve no traveling and considerably less time.

Cocaine – An illegal drug. Also known as "coke" or "blow," cocaine often resembles a white crystalline or powdery substance. It is highly addictive and dangerous.

Common Application – An application with which students can apply to multiple schools.

Course Registration – The period of official class selection for the upcoming quarter or semester. Prior to registration, it is best to prepare several back-up courses in case a particular class becomes full. If a course is full, students can place themselves on the waitlist, although this still does not guarantee entry.

Division Athletics – Athletic classifications range from Division I to Division III. Division IA is the most competitive, while Division III is considered to be the least competitive.

Dorm – A dorm (or dormitory) is an on-campus housing facility. Dorms can provide a range of options from suite-style rooms to more communal options that include shared bathrooms. Most first-year students live in dorms. Some upperclassmen who wish to stay on campus also choose this option.

Early Action – An application option with which a student can apply to a school and receive an early acceptance response without a binding commitment. This system is becoming less and less available.

Early Decision – An application option that students should use only if they are certain they plan to attend the school in question. If a student applies using the early decision option and is admitted, he or she is required and bound to attend that university. Admission rates are usually higher among students who apply through early decision, as the student is clearly indicating that the school is his or her first choice.

Ecstasy – An illegal drug. Also known as "E" or "X," ecstasy looks like a pill and most resembles an aspirin. Considered a party drug, ecstasy is very dangerous and can be deadly.

Ethernet – An extremely fast Internet connection available in most university-owned residence halls. To use an Ethernet connection properly, a student will need a network card and cable for his or her computer.

Fake ID – A counterfeit identification card that contains false information. Most commonly, students get fake IDs with altered birthdates so that they appear to be older than 21 (and therefore of legal drinking age). Even though it is illegal, many college students have fake IDs in hopes of purchasing alcohol or getting into bars.

Frosh – Slang for "freshman" or "freshmen."

Hazing – Initiation rituals administered by some fraternities or sororities as part of the pledging process. Many universities have outlawed hazing due to its degrading, and sometimes dangerous, nature.

Intramurals (IMs) – A popular, and usually free, sport league in which students create teams and compete against one another. These sports vary in competitiveness and can include a range of activities—everything from billiards to water polo. IM sports are a great way to meet people with similar interests.

Keg – Officially called a half-barrel, a keg contains roughly 200 12-ounce servings of beer.

LSD – An illegal drug, also known as acid, this hallucinogenic drug most commonly resembles a tab of paper.

Marijuana – An illegal drug, also known as weed or pot; along with alcohol, marijuana is one of the most commonly-found drugs on campuses across the country.

Major –The focal point of a student's college studies; a specific topic that is studied for a degree. Examples of majors include physics, English, history, computer science, economics, business, and music. Many students decide on a specific major before arriving on campus, while others are simply "undecided" until declaring a major. Those who are extremely interested in two areas can also choose to double major.

Meal Block – The equivalent of one meal. Students on a meal plan usually receive a fixed number of meals per week. Each meal, or "block," can be redeemed at the school's dining facilities in place of cash. Often, a student's weekly allotment of meal blocks will be forfeited if not used.

Minor – An additional focal point in a student's education. Often serving as a complement or addition to a student's main area of focus, a minor has fewer requirements and prerequisites to fulfill than a major. Minors are not required for graduation from most schools; however some students who want to explore many different interests choose to pursue both a major and a minor.

Mushrooms – An illegal drug. Also known as "'shrooms," this drug resembles regular mushrooms but is extremely hallucinogenic.

Off-Campus Housing – Housing from a particular landlord or rental group that is not affiliated with the university. Depending on the college, off-campus housing can range from extremely popular to non-existent. Students who choose to live off campus are typically given more freedom, but they also have to deal with possible subletting scenarios, furniture, bills, and other issues. In addition to these factors, rental prices and distance often affect a student's decision to move off campus.

Office Hours – Time that teachers set aside for students who have questions about coursework. Office hours are a good forum for students to go over any problems and to show interest in the subject material.

Pledging – The early phase of joining a fraternity or sorority, pledging takes place after a student has gone through rush and received a bid. Pledging usually lasts between one and two semesters. Once the pledging period is complete and a particular student has done everything that is required to become a member, that student is considered a brother or sister. If a fraternity or a sorority would decide to "haze" a group of students, this initiation would take place during the pledging period.

Private Institution – A school that does not use tax revenue to subsidize education costs. Private schools typically cost more than public schools and are usually smaller.

Prof – Slang for "professor."

Public Institution – A school that uses tax revenue to subsidize education costs. Public schools are often a good value for in-state residents and tend to be larger than most private colleges.

Quarter System (or Trimester System) – A type of academic calendar system. In this setup, students take classes for three academic periods. The first quarter usually starts in late September or early October and concludes right before Christmas. The second quarter usually starts around early to mid–January and finishes up around March or April. The last academic quarter, or "third quarter," usually starts in late March or early April and finishes up in late May or Mid-June. The fourth quarter is summer. The major difference between the quarter system and semester system is that students take more, less comprehensive courses under the quarter calendar.

RA (Resident Assistant) – A student leader who is assigned to a particular floor in a dormitory in order to help to the other students who live there. An RA's duties include ensuring student safety and providing assistance wherever possible.

Recitation – An extension of a specific course; a review session. Some classes, particularly large lectures, are supplemented with mandatory recitation sessions that provide a relatively personal class setting.

Rolling Admissions – A form of admissions. Most commonly found at public institutions, schools with this type of policy continue to accept students throughout the year until their class sizes are met. For example, some schools begin accepting students as early as December and will continue to do so until April or May.

Room and Board – This figure is typically the combined cost of a university-owned room and a meal plan.

Room Draw/Housing Lottery – A common way to pick on-campus room assignments for the following year. If a student decides to remain in university-owned housing, he or she is assigned a unique number that, along with seniority, is used to determine his or her housing for the next year.

Rush – The period in which students can meet the brothers and sisters of a particular chapter and find out if a given fraternity or sorority is right for them. Rushing a fraternity or a sorority is not a requirement at any school. The goal of rush is to give students who are serious about pledging a feel for what to expect.

Semester System – The most common type of academic calendar system at college campuses. This setup typically includes two semesters in a given school year. The fall semester starts around the end of August or early September and concludes before winter vacation. The spring semester usually starts in mid-January and ends in late April or May.

Student Center/Rec Center/Student Union – A common area on campus that often contains study areas, recreation facilities, and eateries. This building is often a good place to meet up with fellow students; depending on the school, the student center can have a huge role or a non-existent role in campus life.

Student ID – A university-issued photo ID that serves as a student's key to school-related functions. Some schools require students to show these cards in order to get into dorms, libraries, cafeterias, and other facilities. In addition to storing meal plan information, in some cases, a student ID can actually work as a debit card and allow students to purchase things from bookstores or local shops.

Suite – A type of dorm room. Unlike dorms that feature communal bathrooms shared by the entire floor, suites offer bathrooms shared only among the suite. Suite-style dorm rooms can house anywhere from two to ten students.

TA (Teacher's Assistant) – An undergraduate or grad student who helps in some manner with a specific course. In some cases, a TA will teach a class, assist a professor, grade assignments, or conduct office hours.

Undergraduate – A student in the process of studying for his or her bachelor's degree.

California Colleges

California dreamin'?
This book is a must have for you!

CALIFORNIA COLLEGES
7¼" X 10", 762 Pages Paperback
$29.95 Retail
1-59658-501-3

Stanford, UC Berkeley, Caltech—California is home to some of America's greatest institutes of higher learning. *California Colleges* gives the lowdown on 24 of the best, side by side, in one prodigious volume.

New England Colleges

**Looking for peace in the Northeast?
Pick up this regional guide to New England!**

NEW ENGLAND COLLEGES
7¼" X 10", 1015 Pages Paperback
$29.95 Retail
1-59658-504-8

New England is the birthplace of many prestigious universities, and with so many to choose from, picking the right school can be a tough decision. With inside information on over 34 competive Northeastern schools, *New England Colleges* provides the same high-quality information prospective students expect from College Prowler in one all-inclusive, easy-to-use reference.

Schools of the South

Headin' down south? This book will help you find your way to the perfect school!

SCHOOLS OF THE SOUTH
7¼" X 10", 773 Pages Paperback
$29.95 Retail
1-59658-503-X

Southern pride is always strong. Whether it's across town or across state, many Southern students are devoted to their home sweet home. *Schools of the South* offers an honest student perspective on 36 universities available south of the Mason-Dixon.

Untangling the Ivy League

The ultimate book for everything Ivy!

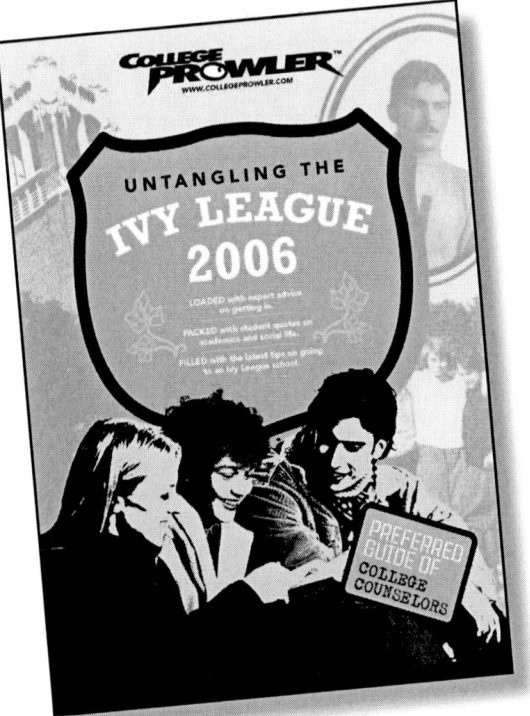

UNTANGLING THE IVY LEAGUE
7¼" X 10", 567 Pages Paperback
$24.95 Retail
1-59658-500-5

Ivy League students, alumni, admissions officers, and other top insiders get together to tell it like it is. *Untangling the Ivy League* covers every aspect—from admissions and athletics to secret societies and urban legends—of the nation's eight oldest, wealthiest, and most competitive colleges and universities.

Need Help Paying For School?

Apply for our scholarship!

College Prowler awards thousands of dollars a year to students who compose the best essays. E-mail scholarship@collegeprowler.com for more information, or call 1-800-290-2682.

Apply now at ***www.collegeprowler.com***

Tell Us What Life Is Really Like at Your School!

Have you ever wanted to let people know what your college is really like? Now's your chance to help millions of high school students choose the right college.

Let your voice be heard.

Check out *www.collegeprowler.com* for more info!

Need More Help?

Do you have more questions about this school? Can't find a certain statistic? College Prowler is here to help. We are the best source of college information out there. We have a network of thousands of students who can get the latest information on any school to you ASAP. E-mail us at info@collegeprowler.com with your college-related questions.

E-Mail Us Your College-Related Questions!

Check out *www.collegeprowler.com* for more details.
1-800-290-2682

Write For Us!
Get published! Voice your opinion.

Writing a College Prowler guidebook is both fun and rewarding; our open-ended format allows your own creativity free reign. Our writers have been featured in national newspapers and have seen their names in bookstores across the country. Now is your chance to break into the publishing industry with one of the country's fastest-growing publishers!

Apply now at **www.collegeprowler.com**

Contact editor@collegeprowler.com or
call 1-800-290-2682 for more details.

Pros and Cons

Still can't figure out if this is the right school for you? You've already read through this in-depth guide; why not list the pros and cons? It will really help with narrowing down your decision and determining whether or not this school is right for you.

Pros	**Cons**
....	....
....	....
....	....
....	....
....	....
....	....
....	....
....	....
....	....
....	....
....	....
....	....
....	....

Pros and Cons

Still can't figure out if this is the right school for you? You've already read through this in-depth guide; why not list the pros and cons? It will really help with narrowing down your decision and determining whether or not this school is right for you.

Pros	**Cons**
....	....
....	....
....	....
....	....
....	....
....	....
....	....
....	....
....	....
....	....
....	....
....	....
....	....

Notes

Notes

Notes

Notes

Notes

Notes

Notes

Notes

Notes

Notes

Notes

Notes

Notes

Notes

Notes

Notes

Notes

Notes

Notes

Notes

Notes

Notes